Becoming the Real BOSS!

PAMELA D. HOGAN

ISBN: 979-8-89663-785-1

Dedication

To my loving mother, my pillar and source of strength. You have guided me through life's challenges and helped me become who I am today. Thank you for your constant love and support.

Acknowledgments

I would like to express my heartfelt gratitude to my husband and steadfast business partner, James Hogan, a devoted father and life partner, and our son, Jordan Hogan. Your support through every step of this journey has been invaluable, and I couldn't have done this without you. To my friends, family, and everyone who has inspired or supported me along the way, thank you for your encouragement and belief in me. This book is a testament to the strength and love you have all provided.

About the Author

Internationally renowned beauty educator, expert and celebrity stylist Pamela D. Hogan has traveled the globe, sharing her expertise with both professionals and consumers in the beauty industry. She has led educational sessions across countries such as the United Kingdom, Nigeria, Trinidad, Senegal, Barbados, Punta Cana, and the Bahamas. Pamela's passion for cosmetology was ignited at the age of 15, and in 1996, she established her first business, Tom

Harris Elite Salons, in Norcross, GA. She later expanded her brand with Atlanta Elite Salon in Houston, TX. Continuing her entrepreneurial journey, she opened Salon Elite in Snellville, GA, in 2005, followed by Xclusive Salon & Spa in 2009. Later opening her chain of Simply Beautiful Salons throughout the state Georgia.

With over 30 years of experience in the beauty industry, Pamela has worked as a master educator for prestigious companies, including L'Oréal, Soft Sheen, and Bronner Brothers. Currently, she serves as a research and development consultant for Strength of Nature, a leading multicultural hair care brand, where she contributes to product formulation and testing for brands like **African Pride, Beautiful Textures, Elasta QP, Mega Growth, Soft & Beautiful, and more.

In 2016, Pamela expanded her expertise by attending the Rodney Barnett School of Trichology, becoming a licensed and certified trichologist. One of her proudest accomplishments is the founding of the Hogan Institute of Cosmetology & Esthetics in 2010. What began with the last $11,000 that Pamela and her husband had to their name has grown into a **Title IV educational institution**, where she mentors and transforms students into skilled beauty professionals. She also serves as a board member of the Vocational Program across Gwinnett County, contributing significantly to educational and career development in the beauty industry. Utilizing her industry knowledge and her husband's carpentry skills, they converted an old post office building in Lilburn, GA, into a thriving million-dollar business.

Pamela's story began in **Troy, Alabama**, where she grew up in the projects of a small town, learning early on the values of hard work and perseverance. Beyond beauty, Pamela Hogan is a philanthropist. She is committed to community service, passionately empowering young women and men to achieve independence and pursue their dreams. Bring one of her live long dreams back to her hometown, she opened her second location in **Troy Alabama.** She option her dual teacher instructor's license in **Georgia and Alabama**.

Her philanthropic efforts include organizing benefit fashion shows for cancer patients and contributing to the **Nina J. Spicer Foundation**, a mentoring program for youth in collaboration with the **Gwinnett County Public School System.**

Contents

Chapter 1: A Boss in the Making

When I was 15 years old, I made a decision that changed my life forever. I knew I never wanted to work for anyone and wanted to be my own boss. At that young age, I had two passions - fashion design and hairstyling. I loved designing and sewing clothes; I was always drawn to anything that involved creativity and design. So, I had to choose between these two career paths.

I was at school in my home economics class when I realized how much I loved fashion. I loved the beauty, the elegance, and the creativity that went into designing clothes. I would spend hours drawing and creating different outfits, imagining myself as a famous fashion designer. But then, I also loved hairstyling. I loved how a great haircut or a perfect hair color could transform someone's entire look. I loved anything that involved making someone feel beautiful and confident.

Then, one day, I met a woman who changed everything. She was a hairstylist at a local salon, and she was stunning. Her hair, clothes, makeup - everything about her was perfect. I didn't know her name at that time, but I knew then that I wanted to be just like her - beautiful, fashionable, and successful.

So, I decided to become a hairstylist. I felt like I could get the best of both worlds - creativity and design and making people feel beautiful and confident. When I was in 10th grade, I decided to join the cosmetology program at the vocational program at my high school. It was a simple program that only cost $90 a year for supplies. My instructor, Ms Meadows, was very kind and mentored me throughout the program.

As I progressed through 10th grade, I felt more confident that becoming a hairstylist was my future. However, during that time, my mother got me a job at a fast-food restaurant called Crow's Chicken. Although it was not related to my dream of becoming a hairstylist, I took the job.

After working there for two weeks, I realized that wiping grease and making coleslaw was not what I wanted to do for the rest of my life. I quit my job that day, and I knew it wasn't the right thing to do since my mother worked for the Crowe family that owned the restaurant, and they were upset with me.

I apologized to Mr. Crowe and thanked him for the opportunity and for helping me with a job. However, I knew that hairstyling was what I wanted to do, so I turned in my uniform and set out to find a salon where I could begin my journey as a hairstylist.

I remember feeling inspired by what I saw. I wanted to be just like those talented hairstylists I had seen. I visited about three salons, trying to find my place in the industry. I worked as an assistant in one salon, but the owner didn't pay me at the end of the week, so I left. Then I found a small salon, and there she was—the same beautiful lady I had seen before. She owned her own salon. The sweet young lady's name was Joanne. Her salon was called New Dimensions, and it only had three stations, and it was perfect. I was drawn to her kindness and soft-spoken nature and decided to work for her as an assistant. After just three days, I had made $100, which was a lot of money for me at the time. I was still attending vocational school, but I learned so much from Joanne that I felt like I was ready to take on my own clients. She must have noticed my hard work because she gave me my own station after a couple of weeks. I was thrilled and proud of myself. I knew I wasn't licensed to do hair, but I felt ready to take on the challenge.

I worked hard to make my clients happy and feel good about themselves. It became a passion of mine, and I grew my business and my clientele. I was proud to be a hairstylist, and I wanted to make Joanne proud, too. It was amazing to see how far I had come, and I knew that this was the career for me.

However, I couldn't shake off the feeling that something was missing in my life. I mean, my business was thriving, and I was making more money than most teenagers. My mom even started giving me bills to pay to teach me responsibility. But still, there was this void that I couldn't fill.

I had a booming clientele, and most of my advertisement was through word of mouth, but I felt like I needed more. I remember thinking, 'Where do I go from here?' I was about to graduate from high school, and I just couldn't find what I needed. It was like there was this nagging feeling inside of me that something else was waiting for me, something that could take my career to the next level. I didn't know what it was yet, but I knew it was out there. I started exploring my options. I researched different places I wanted to move to advance my career and find the best fit for me. And then I found it. I found the perfect place that would take me to where I needed to be. I remember feeling excited and scared at the same time. I remember visiting my aunt, who had moved to Atlanta the year before. Atlanta was a place where all the people were well put together with beautiful clothes and gorgeous hairstyles.

When I graduated from high school, I knew that my next step was to move to Atlanta. It was a decision I had made long before graduation day, despite my mother's concerns about leaving behind a stable client base for my career. I was determined to go to Atlanta to grow and expand my skills. I knew that this was the place where I could thrive and take my career to new heights.

A few months after graduation, I finally got my diploma and was able to send the paperwork to the state board. Ms Meadows, my instructor, had been instrumental in preparing the class for the state board exams. She had drilled us relentlessly and even accompanied us to Montgomery to ensure that we were fully prepared for the process. Thanks to her guidance and support, we all passed on our first attempt. With my license in hand, I was finally able to make the move to Atlanta. It was an exciting time, and I was eager to start my new life there. My cousin had already moved to Atlanta with my best friend, Sharon, and I couldn't wait to join them. We were all young and full of energy, ready to take on the world. I'll never forget the feeling of driving up to the city limits of Atlanta. It was a rush of excitement and anticipation, knowing that I was about to embark on a new adventure. Atlanta was the perfect place for me to start my career, and I was ready to take on whatever challenges came my way.

I lived in an apartment complex where my aunt resided. We used to refer to it as the "Bank head," although it now has a different name. I vividly remember the day my mom drove me there, and as we pulled into the parking lot, chaos unfolded before my eyes. There was a heated altercation, with people yelling and fighting and a crowd gathered around them. I was bewildered, trying to make sense of the situation. It turned out to be a terrible fight between my aunt and her husband, and it was evident that my aunt had suffered abuse. Her face was covered in wounds and bruises, and as an 18-year-old, it was a distressing experience for me. I had come there with excitement and anticipation, only to be thrust into an incident of domestic violence.

The police were called, and my uncle was arrested while my aunt was rushed to the hospital for medical attention. My mother was furious at this point because she never wanted us to be exposed to such a dangerous situation. Additionally, my cousin and my best friend were also present and deeply upset. They had come up there with high hopes and were now confronted with this traumatic event. My mother intervened immediately and declared that we would not be staying there. She was adamant about protecting us from further harm. My mother, always prepared for anything, quickly decided that we would stay in a hotel temporarily while she searched for a new apartment for us. She was determined to find us a safe and separate living space. As we walked out the door, my cousin, my girlfriend, and I, who had all graduated together, said our goodbyes. True to her nature as a caring and compassionate mother, she knew she had to make sure we were safe.

That night, we all stayed together in a hotel. The next day, my mother got up early, and we embarked on the mission of finding a new apartment. Instead of looking for a small one-bedroom unit, my mother sought out a three-bedroom apartment to accommodate all of us. She put down the necessary money, paid the first two months' rent, furnished the place, and even stocked it with groceries. She made sure all the utilities were set up. My mother went above and beyond to ensure the well-being of us girls before leaving for Georgia.

We were immensely grateful to her for her unwavering support. We settled into our new three-bedroom apartment, feeling a sense of independence and readiness to conquer the world. Each of us secured jobs and my first job was at a store called Riches. I still remember the satisfaction of receiving physical receipts, although I'm not sure if they are still used today. Working there was a positive experience, and my girlfriend and cousin also found jobs at the airport in security roles. We were doing well, and the excitement of youth and the enthusiasm for life fueled our spirits. However, about two weeks later, another unfortunate incident occurred involving my aunt. Against everyone's advice, she allowed her husband back into her life, and history repeated itself. He subjected her to another round of abuse, prompting us to call the police once more and have him arrested. It was heartbreaking to witness the impact on my aunt's two young daughters, who were also victims of this cycle of violence. Additionally, another aunt who lived with them sought refuge at our doorstep, frantically knocking for us to let her in.

In Atlanta, I began building my career, starting from the bottom at Riches and working my way up. I was dedicated and focused, always ensuring I was punctual and committed to my work. Eventually, I became a manager and had the opportunity to oversee two stores. However, despite the success, I felt like something was missing. I had a burning desire to be on stage, witnessing the incredible transformations and stunning hairstyles created by talented artists. I wanted to be one of them.

I vividly remember attending a hair show in Atlanta and handing my resume to someone there. It was a small company, not widely known, but I saw it as my chance to become a platform artist and take my career to the next level. From there, I transitioned to working with two or three different companies, continuously moving up the ladder. I aspired to become a business owner and establish my own chain of salons. Determined and ambitious, I set my sights on opening my first salon at the age of 23. To achieve this dream, I educated myself, sought the advice of industry experts, and surrounded myself with like-minded individuals who believed in my vision. I opened Tom Harris Elite, a franchise under another company I had previously worked for. It was a success, and for a few years, I basked in the joy of owning my salon alongside my first husband, who had also been part of Tom Harris Salon.

However, the bliss was short-lived as infidelity entered our marriage. Disheartened, I decided to leave it all behind, including the salon, and start anew in Houston. I sold my house and embarked on a fresh chapter. I knew that as long as I had my talent and skills, I could rebuild my life and make a living anywhere.

***

Houston proved to be an exciting experience; when I searched for work in Houston, I did my homework well. I first chose the right salon, spent some time and money on my portfolio, and made sure to send my bio besides the resume. But unfortunately, sometimes what you go for isn't really what you seek. The business owner I approached happened not to be the person the salon claimed. A number of things besides the owner seemed off to me. And with that, I realized it wasn't even the place for me. At times like this, all you have to do is 'pay attention.' Be cautious of your surroundings, look at things around and listen if you can find a hint. I had been attentive and observant enough to figure out what was wrong. And that's what helped me recognize I wasn't at the right place. So, without wasting much time, I moved on, determined to find the right place to continue my journey and fulfill my aspirations. Meanwhile, our salon in Atlanta, under my ex's supervision, wasn't thriving. Its quality declined day by day, indicating it was time for me to shut it down.

"I know it's getting ready to close its doors," I said, suggesting, "Why don't you give me the furniture? I'm thinking about opening something here?"

"Oh, yeah. You can take that."

With his words, half of my problem was solved. I then bought a place for the salon, and once I had it, my ex's brother helped drive the furniture to me. It was a nice big flat with Italian floors, and the only thing I had to do now was move in the furniture and set it well. As I did everything myself, I ended up opening that salon for $2,500.

Sounds unrealistic! Right? But I did it. I had made a station salon, which included everything: a manicure and pedicure area, a massage room, my office, and so on and so forth. With that wonderful new salon, I initiated the business – all from scratch.

The salon boomed ironically. It was nothing short of a miracle. One after another, my new salon was popular already. I had enough customers that I soon hired full staff. Do you know what's more impressive? We didn't do a single advertisement. Not one. Our salon was located on the major street off Westheimer near the Galleria area and got highlighted on its own for multiple reasons, i.e., the location and the services that complemented its tremendous growth. From there, the business flourished, making me reach new heights.

At that time, I met a young man out of business. The guy was not only smart but also kind and helpful. He assisted me in keeping check and balance on the salon business. That alone was a complex thing to manage, and as he kept doing that for me, I ended up marrying him.

It was a beautiful feeling. The experience of having my husband there to support me whenever I needed it was a blessing, and my husband's skills multifold the profit.

Eventually, I was able to work with L'Oréal, a significant player in the industry. Being one of their regional cosmetologists and platform artists allowed me to travel nationally extensively for several years and expand the business clientele in Houston.

In the next five years, our business thrived in Houston. But despite the success, I found myself missing Atlanta. I felt like I had left the place for the wrong reasons. This strong sense of remorse urged me to go back to Atlanta. I needed to be where my true love (the hair industry) belonged. Though the beauty industry is thriving in Houston, I was missing Atlanta. When I shared my desire to return to Atlanta, I found my husband quite excited. He was born in Houston and never lived in any other place. That's why the idea of moving somewhere else appealed to him. We had to plan and make sure this was the right move for us. We had our son by then, and we had to make sure to take care of him. "I'll be working close to home and family," I had decided before moving back.

In Atlanta, we rented a house for our little family. While staying up there, my husband and I saved enough money to buy us a home. Even though those times were tough, like settling into a new place, I had the desire to reopen my salon there. I didn't like the idea of spending money in a plaza-like in Houston; we had to think smarter.

While aiming for business, I had to invest money, yet invest mindfully. So, rather than putting it in the plaza, I had my eyes on a house on a main highway in Snellville, GA. The day I had the first look at the house on Highway 124, I knew I wanted it. My husband and I put earnest money down and locked the deal in. We closed the next month and had the home in our name.

Once we had the home, we remodeled it as a salon and spa. It was unbelievable. We had that salon working for at least 15 years, through which I built up a long list of clientele and, without a doubt, loads of money. I eventually went on to work for other fluid companies as a platform artist.

One company, in particular, holds a special place in my heart. Mario de la Guardia, the founder, became like a mentor and a guiding force in my life. I have been with this company for over 17 years, and Mario has supported me through thick and thin, even helping me during the development of my future school. Along my journey, I became a senior hairstylist, a national educator, and eventually an international educator, traveling around the world to share my knowledge and skills with this company. However, I felt the urge to grow further as I reached the global stage. At the time, I wasn't sure where my path would lead, but I knew I wanted to mentor others. Many young girls sought my guidance, but I hesitated, feeling the need to continue my own ascent.

Later, after working consistently for a decade, one day, I said, "I feel like I'm still missing something."

"What's that?" my husband asked curiously.

"I don't know. I'm doing what I wanted, but still, there is something else for me."

"You always wanted to open up a school. Why don't you go for it?" My husband induced the long-held thought in my mind.

"I am not ready for it yet. Why don't we open a couple more salons?" I put forth the idea, speaking of my vision to have more franchises everywhere.

My husband agreed, and we opened a chain of salons. We went on to inaugurate five salons in different counties. We had the first one in Snellville, then went on to Warner Robins, Stone Mountain, Lilburn, and Lawrenceville. I still remember how dedicatedly I trained all the stylists there myself. Despite introducing five more salons, I was stuck. I found myself still contemplating that thought in school. "What about my own school?" And as I talked about this, my husband said, "You should own a school. You always wanted to do this. I know you have a passion for that, and you should go for it."

"Yeah, I guess now I am ready for this."

Deep inside my heart, besides traveling, I have also always had a passion for education. I served myself with the best combo of two. I traveled across the world; I visited London, Paris, Dubai, Trinidad, Barbados, Africa, and many other places, exploring different educational mediums. My inner self encouraged me to be the teacher, but how could I do that without a license? Despite the doubts and tight schedule, my husband made me visit the school, and together, we worked it out for me.

That's how my journey toward my passion began. I used to go to school twice a week to get a grip on teaching – the career I had newly chosen for myself. Seven months of a hectic routine, managing both the salon and school, eventually led me to my graduation. The day came when I stood holding my teaching license in my hand, "I've made it!"

I was proud of myself. But what now? I never wanted to get employed at someone else's school. My dream wasn't to earn the certificate and become a teacher. I had a bigger vision. What I needed was to have my own school – to create an opportunity for many others. With that in mind, my husband and I had to step out on faith. We had been successful in the beauty industry, and now we were determined to step into the new field of education. And all of this wasn't only the dream goal or passion; it was business! My husband and I had made enough money. And now, it was on us to invest it fruitfully to ensure the cycle of making more money rather than ending up with minimal or none at all.

The process repeated itself with our hands. From finding the location to making it ideal for our business, we were both on a mission to make it a success. We chose an old-fashioned building, which had actually been a post office earlier, and collaborated with its owner to work it out with $11000.00 at hand. The downpayment helped us get it renovated, reaching a point from where we could take a start, at least. I knew starting the business all alone could sink things down the drain. I decided to kick-start the business via partnership.

Luckily, I soon found two young ladies interested in joining hands to run the school. An important thing here is to ensure that they are a suitable fit for my business. One lady already had experience in the school sector, which meant she definitely knew more than me. The other young lady had worked in the financial department of a school. This alone could help us figure out the budget, profit, and loss. But it wasn't as simple as it may sound. Sometimes, when things seem like they're falling in place magically, they can fall apart just as easily. That's what happened to me and my partnership. They were struggling to get their money to together. Stepping back however, couldn't be the only option for me. As my husband was the constructor and one of the partner's husband was the electrician, they together were committed to complete the building projects. This sounded perfect, and my husband and I were all in until we realized it wasn't the whole picture.

Despite the commitment, one of my partners made a point for her husband to be paid for the work he had done, although my husband had done majority of the work. My husband was not getting paid! It was understood that our husbands were committed to the build out on behalf of us as partners. This was unjust and biased, of course! That's what was indicated to my husband and me. We then knew we had to do this journey alone, we had to let them go.

Remember, you don't always get what you want, but at such times, you must know how to make it best for you. Likewise, we now had the building, not the preferred yet suitable enough to open. We had to grow into it, and we did it. Evenly, we completely changed everything, from the floors to the painting on the walls and some structure. All thanks to my husband's construction background, we could figure it out.

With much research and endless nights, we managed to obtain enough knowledge to get licensed as a state cosmetology and esthetics college. Once the school building was furnished, we were officially ready to begin with experience and intellect. As we moved forward, our thoughts were scattered. The plan had almost failed. Yet, I wasn't ready to give up. I knew I could make it, not knowing how. It's true that when you put your heart into something, you make it worth it. This school wasn't merely a side business for me but something I truly wanted. I truly believed what my mother always said; even when doors closed, I kept searching for a window for the light to pierce in, and it eventually did.

I attended seminars, workshops, and events with the intention of interacting and extending my network. I made sure to keep promoting my requirements while learning more about this new business I was indulging myself in.

October 17, 2010, marked the inauguration of the school. My goal was to give back to the community, and seeing myself achieving that goal was priceless.

The grand opening was overwhelming. We invited twelve women as guests from a women's abuse shelter, such as Sister's House, in Atlanta. We were privileged to do their makeover for zero cost. The smiles on their faces and the tears of happiness in their eyes were payment enough. It was so pure and heartwarming. Those women, though abused, were exceptional. Each had their own story to tell, and their endurance was amazing. We made arrangements to take them to the opening event, and they were grateful.

Those broken hearts had spirits within that revived, even if for the time being. This made my emotions flow unlike ever before. This was an example of what I used to do as an artist – work on people's faces to change their appearance and personalities. We make them look like an entirely new person according to how they wanted themselves to be. It isn't just a business or work; it is a form of therapy – a therapy for both the doers and takers. And this is why I always encourage my students to own what they do.

Working in the beauty industry is an art, and one must have passion for it. If you have passion and dedication, the money will follow. Trust me, it is more about doing the best work and doing it correctly. I took both, working at the salon and teaching at the school, hand in hand, only because I was passionate about it and wanted to make it, so I did.

No pretense, managing two things at once is difficult. And at times, it took a toll on me as well. I couldn't manage to work and teach at once. There, I realized how crucial it is to keep up with your sanity. Sometimes, we burn ourselves out from exhaustion. It often happens only because we want to make things work by ourselves, make money and profit, without making our burden fall on any shoulder other than ours. This is where we do it wrong.

It is always better to recognize your potential and make the most of it before you burn out. Yet, there I was, frustrated and done. "I can't do this anymore," I cried, seeing no way out.

I had worked my ass off for years. Now, when I had a running clientele of 20+ years, I would have never wished to fuck up. So, I took time and made a conscious decision. I had to come from behind the chair, but mindfully and with gratitude. As a business owner, I didn't want to shut the door in my client's face. I preferred to celebrate the years of working together and bid farewell nicely. Though the news of me walking away from behind the chair pissed some off, others appreciated my loyalty. And then, even when I had fulfilled my responsibility toward my clients and was ready to retire, I kept my salon open for a couple of years. I didn't abandon my clients even then but directed them to fellow stylists in the salon. I did it willingly and cheerfully, knowing it was I who resigned and not they who switched.

I now had the time to focus on my school. I put in my hundred percent to grow the school from this point onward. Initially, I had been working as the sole teacher of the school for eight or more months since it started. My husband ran the administrative stuff beside me. But now, it was time for our two-member team to grow. It took us a few months to plan and save money to actually hire staff. At this point, all we could pay was school's staff and expenses.

We had to build it from scratch. It wasn't as if we had the financial aid at the time. Remember, financial aid in the United States requires a business to stand on its own minimum for two years. This means even our school had to endure that challenging initial phase on its own to be eligible for the aid. Yet, we remained true to our goal and worked it out. In the meantime, my husband and I didn't stop there. We both continued expanding our skills by learning more. My husband was a mid-level photographer, so he kept polishing his photography skills. Over time, his passion and hard work led him to exclusive clients in the Atlanta area.

One of those clients was the company I worked for many years. Mario, who offered him some photography projects for his product branding.

My husband and I teamed up once again to rock it. I contributed as a stylist, while my husband relied on his photography skills to make it go as perfectly as the client could ever wish. With side skills and part-time work, we made it through challenging times, making and saving money.

The side hustle may seem like an added problem to one's life, but it is worth your time. It is because of our side hustle that we were able to manage our house expenses and never reached the point of giving up on our school business. Our positive attitude and consistent struggle to work and earn drove us to the more clients, one after the other. My husband's photography business grew tremendously. He went on to work for other major companies. It let us grow stronger and more financially stable with time, only to spend more on our business until it pays back twice as much as we had invested.

We had to learn more marketing strategies. One way to attract more clients, business, or money is to the create a major image. The more successful you look, the more people put their trust in your business. So, at a time when our school hadn't even reached the success point, we relied on this method.

We created an image of our school in our surroundings. We made it look good enough for people to get enrolled. As the enrollments began to come in, the school soon got financial aid from the government – a new hope for success. Though the financial aid was a good thing, it happened to be another ballgame in itself. The process was difficult enough that it pushed me to the verge of giving up. After facing a list of trials and assessments that took months, we somehow made it through that horrendous process. By the grace of God, after a three-month-long process, the school received financial aid in 2017. This truly changed the course of its future since we knew the sky was the limit now. The business grew tremendously, and soon, both my husband and I were able to make money. But remember, this hadn't happened overnight. It took us seven years to reach this point where we would earn enough to pay ourselves, to relish the fruits of the seed we had sown years ago.

Starting in 2010, our school and we, as the owners, have faced countless ups and downs. Yet, the thing that lets us thrive is our patience to bear the losses. We continued working on its growth, never feeling as if it was enough. This led us to the opening of our second school in Alabama, my hometown.

Each of us has a special connection with our hometown. That's what I also had and still have. The urge to serve my people drove me back there. I returned to my hometown after decades and ended up opening a school there.

The idea of giving back to my beloved town was heart-filling and satisfying in itself. It brought me the true essence of serving the community and people from the land where I grew up. Yet, the journey didn't end there. Countless ideas kept crossing our minds. We made several new plans and became unstoppable in setting an example for many like you. A few years before opening the Alabama school, I was honored to have my mentor, Joanne, come and enroll as a student instructor at the Georgia campus. Not knowing that when she obtained her dual teacher instructor's license in Georgia and Alabama, she would be a lead instructor at the school in Alabama. Also, to my surprise, my old teacher Ms. Meadow from my high school cosmetology program became another main teacher instructor at the Alabama location. Talk about a full circle!

Chapter 2: Follow Directions

Now that you have a little history of me and how my journey started, it's time to get down to business! Leadership is a multifaceted skill that requires many different qualities, and one of the most essential of these qualities is the ability to follow directions and become a skilled follower. In the journey of becoming a great leader, it may seem counterintuitive to prioritize being a follower, but in reality, learning how to follow is a fundamental aspect of leadership.

To be a successful follower, one must possess certain characteristics such as patience, modesty, and attentiveness. Understanding that people who are unable to follow are typically reticent to gain knowledge and experience can also be a helpful foundation. Developing the capacity to carefully listen to and understand the information around you can help a person become an effective leader. Being able to stay calm and quiet and make sense of all the input one receives is integral for success in this capacity.

In today's ever-evolving business environment, it's effortless to get sidetracked and forget the significance of active listening. Nonetheless, this skill is necessary for those wanting to become successful bosses and managers. Knowing how to grasp, retain, and assess details is primary for making prudent judgments and carrying out successful initiatives. Thus, honing this ability is essential for somebody aspiring to become an exceptional leader.

Key Factors related to leadership skills

Being successful in life often requires possessing leadership skills. These skills consist of having the ability to motivate, direct, and encourage others so that they are able to fulfill a common goal. This book looks into the key elements that help define truly exceptional leaders. It will explore how they communicate, make decisions, and deal with change -- all attributes pertinent to driving positive results for their company or community. Through understanding these basics, people can further enhance their own successes and recognize what is necessary to lead with maximum power and authority.

1. Communication: Effective leadership hinges on strong communication skills. Leaders who excel in this area possess the ability to articulate their thoughts clearly and engage in active listening. This foundational competency is paramount for various reasons, contributing significantly to an organization's success.

Clear communication fosters understanding. When leaders can convey their ideas without ambiguity, it ensures that everyone within the organization comprehends the goals, strategies, and expectations. This clarity prevents misunderstandings, minimizes errors, and reduces conflicts. It creates a shared vision and direction, aligning the team's efforts toward common objectives.

Communication is the cornerstone of effective leadership. Leaders who communicate clearly, listen actively, and build trust through open and honest communication create an environment where teams can thrive. They foster understanding, engagement, and collaboration, ultimately driving the organization toward success. In today's constantly changing and interconnected society, great leaders need to possess the capacity to communicate clearly in order to have a positive effect.

2. Vision: Vision is a fundamental element of effective leadership. It serves as the guiding light, the North Star that leaders use to navigate the turbulent waters of change, inspire their teams, and achieve their goals. Guiding a team with a clear and inspiring vision is crucial for ensuring success; a leader's personal vision provides direction, elicits a clear purpose, and encourages team members. This makes it a fundamental part of successful leadership practices.

Leaders with a clear vision have a powerful tool at their disposal. This vision is a mental image of a desired future state they aspire to create or achieve. It acts as a blueprint, outlining the path toward success. This clarity not only helps leaders set goals but also makes it easier for them to communicate their objectives to their teams.

A clear vision also serves as a unifying force within an organization. It aligns individual and collective efforts toward a common objective. When everyone understands where they are headed, they can work together harmoniously. This alignment fosters a sense of cohesion and teamwork, ultimately enhancing productivity and outcomes.

3. Decision-Making: Decision-making is a fundamental aspect of leadership. It is not just those with charisma or power who are quality leaders; they are those who make good and quick decisions as well. Decision-making is a key feature of effective leaders, as their decisions can heavily affect their organizations. This essay will explain why decision-making is essential for successful leadership and describe the traits that separate great leaders from the rest.

To begin with, good leaders exhibit a keen sense of situational awareness. They are constantly attuned to the ever-changing landscape of their organization or team. This awareness allows them to identify emerging issues, spot opportunities, and anticipate potential challenges. By staying well-informed, leaders are better equipped to make relevant and contextually appropriate decisions. In essence, they do not operate in a vacuum but engage with the dynamic environment they lead.

Decision-making is a cornerstone of effective leadership. Good leaders excel in this domain by maintaining situational awareness, weighing the pros and cons of options, taking calculated risks, and demonstrating decisiveness. These attributes enable leaders to make informed and timely decisions that benefit their organizations or teams. While leadership encompasses a multitude of skills and qualities, the ability to make sound decisions stands out as a defining trait of those who lead with excellence. It is important for potential leaders to understand the importance of making decisions and strive to continually improve their decision-making capabilities.

4. Adaptability: Adaptability is a critical trait for effective leadership in today's fast-paced and ever-changing world. Leaders who possess this quality can navigate uncertainty and thrive in dynamic environments. Adaptability involves a willingness to adjust to new circumstances, embrace change, and remain open to fresh ideas and approaches.

In an era marked by rapid technological advancements and shifting global landscapes, leaders must be prepared to confront unforeseen challenges. These challenges may come in the form of disruptive technologies, economic downturns, or global crises such as the COVID-19 pandemic. Leaders who can adapt swiftly and strategically are better equipped to guide their teams and organizations through such turbulent times.

Adaptable leaders also excel in interpersonal relationships. They are approachable and receptive to feedback from their teams. This openness creates an environment where employees feel valued and empowered. When employees see their ideas being considered and implemented, it boosts morale and encourages them to contribute more actively to the organization's success.

5. Empathy: Empathy is a quality that distinguishes great leaders from those who are merely average. Empathetic leadership consists of the ability to understand and take into consideration the feelings and viewpoints of team members, which leads to the formation of long-term relationships within an organization. This book looks into the importance of empathy in leadership, its effects on team dynamics, and how it fosters success. By embracing empathy, leaders can more effectively enter the world of their team members and look beyond superficial characteristics and identities to find a shared bond. This contributes to developing mutual trust, heightened morale, and a sense of community within the organization. They actively listen, not just to words, but to the underlying emotions and concerns. This skill transcends mere sympathy or surface-level understanding; it is a deep, genuine connection that forms the bedrock of trust and respect.

6. Conflict Resolution: Conflict resolution is a vital skill every leader should possess. In any team or organization, conflicts are bound to arise, whether they stem from differences in opinion, conflicting goals, or interpersonal issues. How a leader handles these conflicts can significantly impact the overall harmony and productivity of the group. Effective conflict resolution requires a combination of communication, empathy, and problem-solving skills.

It's essential for leaders to remain neutral and unbiased when resolving conflicts. Favoritism or taking sides can exacerbate the problem and damage relationships within the team. Leaders should focus on the facts and the best interests of the team or organization as a whole. This impartiality reinforces trust and credibility. In some cases, conflicts may be an opportunity for growth and improvement. Leaders can use conflicts as a catalyst for change by identifying areas that need improvement and implementing necessary changes. Rather than simply restoring things to how they were before, dispute resolution should be seen as an opportunity to strengthen the team or organization and be more able to cope in the future.

7. Delegation: Delegation is an integral aspect of successful leadership and is a key ability that makes or breaks a leader and their staff. It requires assigning jobs and duties to those in the company and providing them the freedom and power needed to do the work properly. While the act of delegation may appear straightforward, its execution is anything but simple. Successful delegation requires a combination of trust, clear communication, and an understanding of one's team members.

Delegation also provides leaders with the opportunity to focus on higher-level responsibilities. Leaders should not only delegate routine or time-consuming tasks but also strategic ones. This way, they will have more time for creating plans, conveying their vision, and growing their team as a whole.

However, delegation is not without its challenges. Leaders must strike a balance between empowerment and oversight. Too much delegation without appropriate supervision can lead to mistakes or a lack of alignment with organizational goals. Consequently, heads ought to create systems for observing advancement and granting assistance if required.

8. Motivation: Effective leadership necessitates strong motivation from leaders to bring out the best performance from their team members. It is essential to understand each team member's unique needs and aspirations and to design motivation strategies tailored to those individual needs. Doing so provides team members with the necessary drive, ambition, and enthusiasm to reach their full potential.

One common approach is to set clear goals and expectations. Leaders should articulate a compelling vision and define achievable objectives, ensuring every team member understands their role in achieving these goals. Clarity empowers individuals by giving them a sense of purpose and direction.

Recognition and rewards also fuel motivation. When leaders acknowledge and celebrate individual and team accomplishments, it reinforces positive behaviors and encourages continued effort. Furthermore, providing opportunities for skill development and growth demonstrates a commitment to personal and professional advancement, motivating team members to invest in their work.

9. Accountability: Accountability is a cornerstone of effective leadership and teamwork. Leaders who embody this trait demonstrate a commitment to owning their actions and choices. They recognize that their choices can cause significant results, both good and bad, and they are content to take up the responsibility that goes along with their occupation.

Moreover, accountable leaders don't stop at personal responsibility. They extend this principle to their team members, fostering a culture of accountability within the group. They make sure that everyone knows what is expected of them, give direction, and guarantee that each individual comprehends their contribution to accomplishing joint objectives.

These leaders recognize that imperfections may come up but consider them as chances for self-improvement and gaining knowledge. When blunders take place, they do not communicate fault or exonerate themselves; rather, they appraise the predicament, recognize areas that need to be better, and make changes to keep the same problem from happening once more.

10. Strategic Thinking: Leaders must possess the capacity to strategically analyze intricate situations, forecast future movements, and make choices that concur with extended ambitions and the major idea of an entity or project.

Individuals who thrive at strategic planning possess the ability to look past the present into the future and contemplate multiple viewpoints. They assess both the hazards and the potential advantages of any specific plan of action and are willing to amend their strategies as needed. Furthermore, they think of the benefits for the long term since they understand that the success of an organization is based on its long-term sustainability. One key aspect of strategic thinking is the ability to identify and prioritize goals. Effective leaders set clear, actionable objectives that move the organization closer to its vision. They also understand that strategic thinking requires ongoing evaluation and adjustment. As the business environment changes, they are ready to pivot and refine their strategies to stay relevant and competitive.

All of these pieces work together to create effective leadership capabilities. It is worth noting that being a leader requires having a wide array of abilities, and different scenarios may necessitate particular features of leadership to stand out.

Throughout my career, I have noted that the ability to attentively listen, take proper notes, and process data are essential skills to have. Putting down thoughts and plans in writing allows one to envision what lies ahead and better comprehend how to attain desired objectives. This precise way of thinking demonstrates how critical it is to be a knowledgeable follower before maneuvering your way into a supervisory role.

Being around people who have similar goals and beliefs is an important part of achieving success. This idea comes from the understanding that no one has all the knowledge and experience needed to succeed on their own. Learning from others who have gone through similar situations can be incredibly helpful. Following the directions of those who have already succeeded in a particular endeavor can help one avoid unnecessary mistakes and save time and energy in the process. Yet, recognizing and building relationships with these people can prove difficult, necessitating thoughtful deliberation about the individuals we welcome into our personal spheres.

In order to achieve our desired level of success, it is crucial to form a network of people who have similar aspirations and ambitions as us. This network can offer us the necessary support and motivation to progress further. However, it is important to note that not everyone we come across will be encouraging or understanding of our goals. Certain individuals may exhibit negativity and discouragement due to jealousy or a lack of comprehension.

It is crucial to understand the importance of separating ourselves from individuals who obstruct our advancement and instead seek out those who sincerely aid and motivate us. Moreover, it is crucial to realize that not all people will remain a constant part of our journey through life. As we mature and progress, we may have to part ways with individuals who no longer share our aspirations and objectives. This is not a rejection of their past importance but rather an acknowledgment that everyone has a role to play and may only be present for a certain period.

Achieving success in life requires a combination of effort, resolve, and finding the right individuals who can offer guidance, backing, and motivation. Surrounding ourselves with like-minded individuals who aspire to similar goals motivates us to advance with assurance and determination. Acquiring thc skill of being a follower is a crucial milestone toward becoming an exemplary leader. Demonstrating humility, patience, and attentiveness is necessary for absorbing, comprehending, and assimilating information.

Throughout my life and career, I have always sought to surround myself with people who share my values and goals. This includes surrounding myself with those with similar mindsets or who have made more progress in their journeys. My constant desire to learn and expand my knowledge motivates me. I recognize that in order to progress in both my personal and professional life, I need the support and guidance of these individuals.

The reason behind my achievements lies in the company I keep - individuals who are not only knowledgeable and triumphant but also selfless with their time and expertise. The secret I've found is that when I am among people who truly love what they do, they are always eager to pass on their wisdom and help others thrive.

Based on what I've noticed, the connections that have been most helpful to me are the ones where there is mutual respect and admiration. When I work together with people who are fully devoted to their own improvement and progress, they are more likely to be encouraging of others who also have the same enthusiasm and commitment.

One of the most fulfilling parts of collaborating with individuals with more knowledge and experience is the feeling of thankfulness and recognition they show when they witness others succeed. By following the advice and guidance of those who have already achieved what I aspire to, I have experienced a deep sense of appreciation and gratitude toward these individuals. Due to my achievements, I have been frequently asked to provide advice and mentorship to others. Although I am always ready to share my expertise and experience, I have come to realize that not everyone is receptive or capable of learning from those who have paved the way. Nonetheless, I am dedicated to imparting my knowledge and experience to others, recognizing the significance it holds in fostering the progress and advancement of individuals, teams, and organizations.

In the modern era, people often associate success with money, and many individuals are constantly working toward achieving financial stability and abundance. However, not everyone understands that true prosperity and achievement go beyond just monetary gain. They are the result of a blend of knowledge, experience, and expertise. This is where the importance of having a mentor becomes relevant.

Let's explore the importance of having a mentor and how it can greatly impact one's path to achievement.

The Power of Mentorship

The dynamic of mentorship involves a knowledgeable person (the mentor) guiding someone with less experience (the mentee). This connection plays a significant role in personal and professional growth, allowing individuals to benefit from the wisdom and expertise gained by others throughout their own life paths. Mentorship isn't just a one-way street where the mentor imparts wisdom to the mentee. It's a dynamic relationship where both parties benefit. The teacher feels happy when they pass on what they know, and the student learns things that can really help them grow quickly.

There are many advantages to having a mentor, such as:

1. Guidance: Mentors are incredibly helpful guides, providing a treasure trove of understanding to assist people in navigating the intricacies of life. With their seasoned wisdom, mentors empower mentees to confront challenges and make well-informed decisions. By drawing from their own experiences, mentors serve as beacons of knowledge, illuminating the path to success. They not only share successes but also reveal failures, helping mentees sidestep common pitfalls. Whether in personal relationships, career pursuits, or personal growth, mentors provide a steady hand and a compassionate ear. In the mentor-mentee dynamic, invaluable life lessons are exchanged, enabling individuals to make the best choices aligned with their unique aspirations.

2. Networking: Mentors wield a powerful asset in their mentorship arsenal: networking. These seasoned guides come equipped with vast professional networks cultivated over years of experience. This treasure trove of connections becomes a gateway for mentees, leading to opportunities otherwise hidden. Whether it's introducing mentees to industry experts, potential employers, or like-minded peers, mentors expand horizons. They create bridges, shortening the path to success. These introductions may spark collaborations, job offers, or valuable insights that propel mentees forward. In today's interconnected world, a mentor's network is like a golden key, unlocking doors to knowledge, growth, and professional achievement.

3. Accountability: Having a mentor can provide a sense of accountability. Knowing that someone you respect is watching your progress can be a powerful motivator to stay on track.

4. Emotional Support: Mentorship fosters accountability, a cornerstone of personal and professional growth. When you have a mentor, there's an implicit commitment to progress, and this accountability fuels motivation. The knowledge that a respected figure is observing your journey keeps you accountable to your goals and deadlines. This awareness prevents procrastination and encourages consistency in your efforts. It's akin to having a coach on the sidelines, pushing you to perform your best. This sense of responsibility can drive individuals to exceed their own expectations, ultimately leading to more substantial achievements and a deeper sense of accomplishment in one's endeavors.

5. Skill Development: Mentors play a pivotal role in skill development. They provide invaluable insights and practical advice to catalyze personal and professional growth. Whether it's honing leadership acumen, refining problem-solving abilities, or mastering the art of communication, mentors are seasoncd guides. They share their experiences and techniques, offering a roadmap to success. Mentorship fosters a dynamic exchange of knowledge, where mentees learn from real-world examples and avoid common pitfalls. Through constructive feedback and encouragement, mentors nurture talent and help mentees unlock their full potential. Learning under the guidance of a mentor helps individuals develop their skills and empowers them to excel in their chosen fields by transforming their experience.

Finding the Right Mentor

Having a mentor is extremely important. It's not simply about picking someone who has achieved success; it's about finding a person whose beliefs, values, and past match your ambitions. Here are a few suggestions to assist you in finding the perfect mentor:

1. Identify Your Goals: Having well-defined objectives is the key to developing oneself both personally and professionally. To embark on a successful mentorship journey, it's vital to first identify these goals. Short-term aspirations, like improving a skill, should align with your long-term vision, such as career advancement. This clarity serves as your compass when seeking a mentor. To succeed in a particular area, find a mentor who is knowledgeable in that field. On the other hand, if personal growth is what you're aiming for, a mentor who is good with people could be the perfect choice. Understanding your objectives not only streamlines the mentor selection process but also ensures the mentorship aligns with your aspirations.

2. Research Potential Mentors: When striving for personal and professional growth, one essential step is to research potential mentors. Seek out individuals who have accomplished what you aspire to achieve, whether within your industry, community, or even in unrelated fields. Dive into their work, exploring books, articles, or interviews to gain insights into their philosophies and values. This research isn't merely about emulating their success but understanding the principles that guided them. Doing so allows you to mold your own path, drawing inspiration and wisdom from their experiences. Effective mentorship, even if indirect through their work, can significantly accelerate your journey toward your goals.

3. Network: Networking is a crucial aspect of career growth. Attending conferences, seminars, or workshops within your field is a fantastic way to expand your professional network. These events gather like-minded individuals, offering ample opportunities to meet potential mentors who can guide you in your career journey.

Moreover, consider joining professional organizations specific to your industry. These associations provide a platform for connecting with experienced individuals who can share valuable insights and advice. Online forums are another avenue for networking, especially in today's digital age. Engage in discussions and establish meaningful connections with professionals who have a well of knowledge to offer. Building a robust network can open doors to new opportunities and foster career development.

4. Reach Out: When seeking mentorship, proactive outreach can be your key to success. Don't hesitate; instead, send a well-crafted email or message to potential mentors. In your correspondence, be polite and concise, respecting their valuable time. Clearly articulate your goals and express your admiration for their work. Personalize your message, showcasing a genuine interest in their expertise. Highlighting why you believe their guidance is crucial to your journey sets a strong foundation. Remember, specificity is vital—clarify what you seek from the mentorship. By taking this proactive approach, you show your commitment and increase the likelihood of connecting with mentors who can truly make a difference in your professional growth.

5. Mutual Benefit: Mentorship thrives on mutual benefit. In addition to what you can receive, it's important to consider what you can contribute to your mentor. This mutually beneficial relationship goes both ways. Beyond seeking guidance and wisdom, consider how you can reciprocate. Perhaps you can provide valuable assistance on a project, introduce your mentor to your network, or offer a fresh perspective on their work. These contributions not only enrich your mentor's experience but also strengthen the bond between you. Remember, mentorship is a partnership where both sides contribute, creating a dynamic exchange of knowledge and support that benefits everyone involved.

6. Compatibility: Compatibility is paramount in mentorship. Establishing a strong, personal connection between mentor and mentee is essential for a fruitful journey. The mentor-mentee dynamic thrives when there's a natural personality fit. It's vital to feel at ease when sharing your challenges and seeking guidance. This comfort fosters open communication, enabling you to discuss your professional concerns openly and honestly. Compatibility isn't just about shared interests; it extends to trust, respect, and understanding. When these elements align, mentorship becomes a safe space for growth and learning, where both parties can contribute their best selves and make the most of this invaluable relationship.

7. Commitment: Mentorship thrives on commitment, transcending a mere one-time encounter. It thrives on the enduring relationship built through dedication from both mentor and mentee. This commitment is a pledge to invest not just time but also unwavering effort. It's a recognition that growth and learning take time and perseverance. A mentor must allocate moments of wisdom and guidance consistently, offering valuable insights. Likewise, the mentee must actively seek guidance, absorb knowledge, and implement lessons into their journey. In this ongoing partnership, both parties share responsibility, nurturing growth and fostering a connection that benefits them both. In mentorship, commitment is the cornerstone of success.

When striving for success, it is important to possess both the ability to follow well and actively search for guidance from experienced individuals. Being receptive to acquiring knowledge from those who have already accomplished what you desire can help you save time, prevent avoidable errors, and offer invaluable perspectives that can drive you closer to your objectives.

The Evolving Landscape of Leadership

Leadership is a dynamic idea that changes as time goes on and situations change. While the basic qualities of a good leader stay the same, the methods of exercising leadership have adjusted to fit the modern world.

Leaders are confronted with distinct obstacles in the present-day, fast-moving, globally-connected, and technology-oriented milieu. They must successfully steer through a constantly evolving corporate terrain, make prompt choices, and effectively oversee diverse teams that extend across various time zones and cultures. This necessitates leaders to possess greater agility, adaptability, and receptiveness to new ideas compared to previous times.

Leaders are now no longer anticipated to possess all the solutions. On the other hand, their worth lies in their capacity to promote teamwork, foster innovation, and utilize the combined knowledge of their workforce. This change from conventional, authoritative leadership to more cooperative and inclusive leadership approaches has led to the emergence of the "servant leader" concept - an individual who prioritizes the welfare of their team members and empowers them to achieve greatness.

Mentorship in the Digital Age

In the age of technology, mentorship has evolved to incorporate different methods of communication and learning. Although traditional in-person mentorship is still important, it is not the only choice anymore. Digital mentorship, through video conferencing, messaging apps, and online learning platforms, has gained popularity and is easily accessible.

Digital mentorship offers several advantages:

1. **Global Reach:** With the click of a button, you can connect with mentors from around the world. This expanded reach means you can find mentors with highly specialized expertise that might not be available locally.
2. **Flexibility:** Digital mentorship doesn't require physical proximity, making it easier to schedule meetings and collaborate across time zones. This flexibility is particularly valuable for individuals with busy schedules.
3. **Diverse Perspectives:** Digital mentorship offers the opportunity to tap into a diverse array of viewpoints and encounters. Through connecting with mentors from various fields, cultures, and backgrounds, you can expand your horizons and enhance your understanding.
4. **Resource Sharing:** Sharing articles, videos, and documents has become effortless due to the

convenience offered by online platforms. Mentors can provide valuable learning materials to support your growth.

5. **Recorded Sessions:** Digital mentoring sessions can be recorded, allowing you to revisit and review the advice and insights shared by your mentor. This can be especially helpful for complex topics.
6. **Online Communities:** There are various online groups and platforms where people come together to help and share information. These communities allow you to connect with experienced mentors and individuals who have similar interests, providing you with advice and assistance. It is crucial to have the same dedication and regard for digital mentorship as you would for face-to-face mentorship. Developing a solid digital mentorship bond involves effective communication, attentive listening, and a willingness to dedicate time and energy to the relationship.

The Lifelong Journey of Learning and Leading

Becoming a successful leader involves continuously learning and adapting. The journey to leadership starts by being a skilled follower, which means humility, patience, and attention. Learning from others and absorbing their knowledge and experience can lay a solid foundation for future success.

Mentorship, in both traditional and digital formats, plays a crucial role in this process. It provides guidance, support, and a plethora of valuable insights that can drive individuals closer to their goals in both their personal and professional lives. As the leadership landscape keeps evolving, the capacity to actively pursue and gain from mentorship is a valuable skill that can determine whether one remains stagnant or experiences growth.

Accept and appreciate the changing aspects of being a leader, and be receptive to the transformative influence of guidance and support as you continuously learn and guide others. By doing this, you will not only attain your objectives but also have a positive impact on the progress and advancement of those close to you, causing a widespread influence of leadership and mentorship in your community and beyond.

Take in mentorship not only for its monetary gains but also for its ability to give you a wealth of knowledge, acumen, and personal connections. Foster an environment of serenity, respect, and solicitude as you make strides in becoming a mentor and a student, and always welcome the transformative power of guidance in your voyage toward prosperity. A popular misunderstanding is that having a mentor means handing over money in return for their expertise. While this may be applicable in particular instances, the real worth of mentoring comes from the understanding and background they bring. Numerous hugely successful people, even millionaires and billionaires, attribute their accomplishments to their tutors. This attests to the idea that having a coach does not always equate to financial rewards; it involves learning precious comprehension, capabilities, and experience that can dramatically improve your life and those of others.

When looking for someone to mentor you, it is very important to have the right attitude. Showing humility and eagerness to learn are key. Prioritizing knowledge over financial gain is key, and investing time and effort into the mentorship process is paramount.

It is essential to acknowledge that most mentors are not necessarily driven by financial reimbursement. Many are sincerely hoping to assist you in accomplishing your objectives and wishes. They are eager to watch you succeed and are willing to go above and beyond to give you assistance as desired.

A leader needs to have a combination of characteristics that involve the capacity for learning with others, being patient, humble, and paying close attention. Listening carefully while comprehending and advancing is essential for leading in a fast-moving market.

It is incredibly important to create a community of individuals who encourage you toward your objectives and share the same beliefs as you. It is just as critical, though, to disconnect yourself from those who impede your advancement. Recognizing that not everyone will be a lifelong. Successful people view it as their responsibility to pass along their skills, knowledge, and experience to new generations. They recognize the abundance of wealth and opportunity that exists in the world and are more than happy to share their expertise to help individuals reach their goals.

Getting involved in a mentorship relationship is an important part of establishing your personal and professional growth. It involves gaining valuable wisdom, abilities, and experiences that can support you in leading a successful life. To make this connection with a mentor, display respect, demonstrate your eagerness to learn, and show that you are willing to invest your time and energy in the partnership. Bear in mind understanding is the most precious resource and the right mentor can give you the keys to success.

Beginning one's venture toward success necessitates having a receptive attitude and being ready for the sacrifices that will be encountered along the way. Be aware that there will be occasions when you must do uncomfortable tasks that you may not be initially willing to do. During these times, you should find the strength within you to continue.

In order to reach your objectives, you have to be ready to devote your energy, your perseverance, and everything you have. Realize that making some compromises is necessary in order to accomplish what you want. If you are not eager to carry this out, it would be wise to remain where you currently are and not even try. Nothing of value is ever handed to you; it must be earned. This means putting in effort, persevering, and working hard. Although something that can be achieved effortlessly is not usually held in as much regard as something attained through great difficulty and determination. It is essential to be aware of this fact and strive for that which you desire. Dealing with challenges is a normal part of achieving success. It's important to remain focused on the next step and not let setbacks hold you back. In these tough times, you may come across individuals willing to offer assistance and be there for you. Make the most of this opportunity and reach out for their support.

It is crucial to maintain humility and avoid considering oneself superior to others. When seeking guidance or leadership, being receptive and willing to obey instructions is essential. This principle applies to both leaders and business owners. To achieve success, one must be open to learning from others, paying heed to their advice, and adhering to their guidance.

Achieving success can be challenging, but it is possible for anyone. It requires making sacrifices, putting in effort, and staying determined when faced with challenges. Although the path may be tough, the benefits and fulfillment gained from reaching your objectives are priceless. Therefore, it is important to keep an open mind, stay humble, and maintain a willingness to learn. In doing so, everything else will naturally come together. In my experience as a mentor to students in the beauty industry, there have been instances where I have encountered the challenge of providing a limited amount of guidance and support. Despite their initial eagerness and commitment to succeed, some individuals I have mentored have strayed significantly from the path we had originally agreed upon. When this occurs, I always ensure that I effectively and politely convey that I am no longer able to continue mentoring them. It is not a matter of me giving up on them but rather a realization that their objectives and expectations have become so different from what I can offer that it is beneficial for both parties to go their separate ways.

When I find a student interested in receiving my guidance, the outcomes are often wonderfully gratifying. Seeing them flourish and become accomplished in their occupation is incredibly rewarding. I take pride in the knowledge that several of my protégés have become successful in their field, part of which I like to think is down to the aid and leadership I have given. I must confess that I have also been motivated by the mentors I had when starting my career.

I believe it is essential for mentors to foster an upbeat and encouraging attitude when guiding mentees through their careers in the beauty industry. I aim to show the potential opportunities they have and not let them become discouraged by the difficulties they come across. As such, I implore them to maintain a positive mindset and work diligently in order to achieve their goals. With commitment and dedication, anyone can have a successful and lucrative career in this field. Choosing to live a positive life is one of the most important decisions you'll ever make. No matter where you go or what you do, there will always be naysayers, those who will try to bring you down and fill you with doubts and negativity. However, these people shouldn't deter you from achieving your dreams or reaching the next level. Instead, you should remain positive and focus on the end goal.

It's vital to stay away from people who are negative or toxic. Surround yourself with individuals who share your vision and aspirations. These individuals will be the catalysts that propel you to new heights, especially when you are climbing the ladder toward your ultimate goal. As you continue to grow, your dreams will become a reality, and more importantly, you will find that you are influencing others to grow as well.

Reading and listening to positive materials is another way to maintain focus and positive energy. Listening to motivational tapes, reading inspirational books, and surrounding yourself with like-minded individuals will help provide a positive feedback loop. You will be inspired to keep pushing toward your goals, and the cycle of success will continue.

Throughout your journey, it's important to keep your eyes on the prize. Focus on your ultimate goal and stay committed to achieving it. As you work toward your objectives and reach milestones, you will find that the negative individuals around you will begin to take notice of your success. Even if they don't, that's okay; as long as you remain positive, you will continue to thrive.

Additionally, maintaining a positive mindset is paramount to achieving your most significant aspirations. Remember to distance yourself from negative or toxic people and surround yourself with individuals who share your vision. Stay inspired by reading and listening to positive materials, and always remember to keep your eyes on the prize. When you do this, achieving your goals and success will be within your grasp.

Chapter 3: The Roadmap to Success

The roadmap to success is a critical path that leads individuals to achieve their goals. This requires taking deliberate steps, making significant choices, and following the essentials of the way chosen. Writing down and visualizing ideas and planning out their course provides an understanding of every person's one-of-a-kind trip. Individuals can use this guide to pinpoint the tools and knowledge required for each phase of their journey in order to successfully navigate it.

Prior to taking any action, it is crucial to document all required tasks to achieve one's goals. By doing so, the path becomes clearer, and organizing and executing each step becomes more manageable. Creating a visual representation of this journey will inspire the imagination and help people bring their aspirations to fruition.

Believing in oneself is crucial when working toward achieving set goals. Each day, individuals must remind themselves to come closer to their dream and believe they can achieve it.

This belief drives the determination that is necessary when tackling obstacles along the way. It is equally important for individuals to be their biggest cheerleaders, trusting and affirming that they can succeed despite obstacles that may arise. One must remain determined throughout the journey toward achieving their set goal, ignoring all options and obstacles that attempt to deter them.

Reaching success necessitates having a plan, preparing adequately, and exercising regular determination, self-assurance, order, and discipline. Achieving the desired result requires you to concentrate on the end goal, plan the course, picture it, and remain resolved in spite of the difficulties that come up. It is crucial to keep thorough records, which help keep the attention on track and provide clarity while attempting to meet set objectives.

At times, we may feel caught in a deadlock and that there is no escape. It can appear like everything is against us, and nothing is working out in our favor. It's difficult to sustain enthusiasm when an infinite range of issues present themselves. Nevertheless, we mustn't quit. We need to carry on driving ourselves to reach new heights.

The path to achieving our goals is led by steadfast resolution. We need to trust in our skills and be sure that we will eventually reach our objectives. Even when others may doubt us or tough circumstances arise, our determination must be unyielding. With tenacity and strength, any problem we confront can be conquered.

It is essential to be aware that achieving accomplishments does not happen all of a sudden. Sometimes, it requires a long and difficult path to get to our desired outcomes. We should have faith that the universe will support us and that our exertions will eventually be rewarded. To stay concentrated on our objectives, we have to create a strategy. Writing down our ambitions and actively looking at them can help motivate us to strive to get closer to them. Furthermore, it is crucial to foster a hopeful attitude. Even in times where results do not happen immediately, we have to continue to be optimistic and trust that we will eventually be successful. The most triumphant people in life testify that dedicating yourself and perseverance are the parameters of attaining greatness. They had to forego certain things and invest a manifold of labor to reach their current achievement. Despite this, they never relinquished their inner confidence or their ambitions.

Triumph necessitates resolve, perseverance, and hard work. Maintaining focus on our objectives is paramount, even if they appear impossible to achieve. Staying positive, having a thoughtful strategy, and being prepared to put in the effort can lead to the realization of our ambitions. Keep moving forward with confidence, for success lies ahead for those who seek it.

Commencing a journey toward success is unquestionably demanding, and those who make it seem effortless have likely endured a challenging struggle. Others cannot comprehend the countless hurdles you have already confronted and the ones that await you ahead. Nevertheless, you must persevere and push forward with your dreams. After putting them down on paper and envisioning them, the subsequent step is to take action. Following your plan, which explicitly outlines your goals, is vital in keeping you on course. Moving forward is critical; you must do so with motion and positivity. Many people possess brilliant ideas and dreams, yet they fail to act upon them. These individuals simply ruminate on their thoughts, never jotting them down or visualizing them. Not having enough drive to make progress and failing to come up with a feasible plan to accomplish goals are obstacles to achieving success. It's important to actively strive for your goals and maintain a positive mindset if you want to achieve them. Achieving growth requires dedication and commitment. You must continually work on yourself as well as your objectives. Not prioritizing them can hinder your progress and ambitions from becoming a reality. Thus, it is crucial to invest your time and effort into cultivating positivity and staying focused on your objectives.

Maintaining a hopeful perspective is crucial in reaching your objectives. It is crucial to confront challenges with an optimistic disposition, recognizing that setbacks are mere temporary impediments. Maintaining a happy outlook can seem difficult sometimes, but it will boost your drive and help you stay focused on your goals.

Success is difficult to attain, but persistence, dedication, and optimism can help achieve it. Dedication to a plan, staying focused, and adaptability in tough situations are crucial. By remaining steadfast and optimistic, triumph is attainable.

It's crucial to maintain a hopeful perspective even when faced with hardships since it's simple to fall into pessimism, but it's necessary to break free from that pattern. Negativity will only breed more negativity and hinder our progress. In order to remain optimistic, it's important to maintain focus on personal goals and the journey ahead. Having a positive outlook can boost one's drive and perseverance, which in turn can assist in surmounting obstacles. It's important to recognize that life has its imperfections. Nonetheless, it's crucial to persist regardless of any setbacks.

Every person must take charge of motivating themselves and persist with dedication toward their objectives despite any negative opinions or doubts from others. Consistently using affirmative self-talk and highlighting one's own strengths and abilities is crucial for success. A positive attitude is a continuous journey that demands hard work and perseverance, but its fulfillment can bring about substantial benefits. Concentrating on the favorable can attract optimistic energy and promising chances that can lead us toward accomplishing our goals. So, choose optimism and continue progressing toward the life you aspire to have.

The importance of being around people who share your positive outlook and goals has already been highlighted in chapter two. Having such a network is essential for success. Although there may be times when you feel like quitting, it's imperative to stay focused on the end goal and not give up. With this mindset, there's only room to move forward through steady effort and resolve.

It can be tough when those close to you lack confidence in your ability to succeed, but it's crucial to believe in yourself and remain determined to overcome any doubt. People who share similar principles and are driven by goals will readily offer a helping hand when needed. To attain success, it's important to be receptive to advice and stay humble. To make progress toward your objectives, focus on personal growth and refuse to let negative thoughts hold you back. Creating a positive attitude and connecting with people who share your outlook is key to succeeding.

Believing in yourself, never giving up, and seeking help when needed are also critical elements to master. Make sure to maintain your focus, put in effort, and aim for self-improvement every single day.

Avoiding procrastination is crucial as it can rob you of your valuable time, which cannot be replaced or purchased. From a young age, my mother emphasized the significance of time management, reminding us that time equals money. This adage simply highlights the value of time. Therefore, don't just commit your dreams and goals to paper - take action and start working toward achieving them today. Always remember, tomorrow is not promised to anyone.

You possess the necessary expertise, competencies, and guidelines to prosper. Advance at a steady pace in the direction of your destination. It is the moment to progress forward with unflinching resolve and focus on your objectives. This is the sole verified method to achieving your visions and obtaining your objectives.

It is imperative to stay genuine to who you are as you embark on your journey. This necessitates keeping your promises to both yourself and others. Your promises hold great importance, and it is crucial to fulfill them. Additionally, it is significant to establish daily targets and objectives. It is easy to forget these things, so it's advisable to note them down. Putting thoughts into writing reinforces their importance and enhances the likelihood of actualizing them.

It's common to feel daunted by the number of things on your to-do list. Don't hesitate to inquire or investigate as needed. You can find a wealth of information online to assist you in achieving your objectives. Regardless, remember that triumphing in anything necessitates persistence, effort, and dedication. A few tasks may prove more formidable than others, but it's essential to push ahead and remain resolute in the pursuit of your aspirations.

In the end, if you don't strive toward fulfilling your aspirations and put in effort to achieve them, you are only imagining them. Success can only be attained by writing down your goals and taking steps toward accomplishing them. The journey may be difficult, but every step brings you closer to achieving your dreams. So, work hard, remain committed to your vision, and triumph will come.

Aspire toward fulfilling your dreams and goals with perseverance and a positive attitude. It's time to take that initial step toward success by putting your ideas into action. The worst outcome would be to remain stagnant and consistently ponder the same old dreams from years prior.

Far too often, people have marvelous ideas and ideas they talk about endlessly but never with any real intent to execute them. As a consequence, others who hear these ideas initiate action and utilize them to their advantage. The mediocrity lies within not making any effort to move forward but rather remaining stuck in a perpetual dream state.

Motivation is necessary to advance in the direction of your dreams and goals. There will inevitably be times when hunger and desperation drive you. However, it's important to handle it positively and ethically.

Hunger should never be utilized against others but rather as a motivating tool to further advance your objective. It's important to remember to remain ethical and never burn bridges in pursuit of your dreams.

Achieving your dreams may require effort and determination, but keeping a positive attitude and taking the necessary steps can lead to success. Your aspirations may become a reality in the future.

Attaining a sense of fulfillment through success is a common goal, but it's important to acknowledge that the path to success is often not a simple one and can have negative repercussions in the form of negative karma if taken dishonestly or unethically. Thus, it's vital to prioritize honesty and ethics in the pursuit of success.

Steps And Principles Toward Success

Success is not a random occurrence; it's the result of specific steps and principles. Setting clear and well-defined goals, believing in yourself, meticulous planning, persistence, maintaining a positive outlook, surrounding yourself with support, ethical pursuit, and expressing gratitude are the foundational steps. Let's delve deeper and understand them in detail:

1.Setting Clear Goals

The foundation of any successful endeavor lies in setting clear and well-defined goals. These objectives act as the guiding stars in the night sky, illuminating your path and giving your efforts purpose. But it's not enough to merely harbor these goals in your mind; they must be committed to paper. By documenting your objectives, you create a tangible roadmap for your success. This method not only increases understanding but also increases responsibility. Additionally, listing your objectives in words gives them life and makes them seem more achievable.

2.Belief in Oneself

Have faith in yourself and know that you can achieve greatness. Believing in yourself provides the foundation for reaching any goal you set your sights on. Overcome any difficulties and be strong during hard times. Start each day dedicated to your dreams and recognizing your full potential. Advocate for yourself, be your own motivator, and stand firm when the going gets tough. Trust that you have the ability to make your goals a reality.

3.Planning and Preparation

Success is not something that just happens; it is the result of careful strategizing and hard work. To make it, you have to keep your eyes on the final goal and break it up into steps, achievable goals. Staying resolute is key even when you face challenges. Maintaining documents of your progress is very important as it can help you to remain concentrated and keep a sensible view of your objectives. Keep in mind that an organized plan is like a compass, pointing you in the correct direction when you are not sure and anchoring you when you are experiencing difficulties.

4.Persistence and Perseverance

Achieving success is not a straight path; instead, it is similar to a winding mountain trail. Victory is not given to those who merely wish for it but rather to those who demonstrate relentless dedication, a deep longing for diligent labor, and an unshakeable belief in their capacity. History's most celebrated individuals faced a barrage of obstacles, yet they never surrendered their confidence or ambition. In times of doubt or despair, let your persistence be the wind that fills your sails and propels you forward.

5.Maintaining a Positive Outlook

A positive attitude is the elixir of success. The power to push on through and to confront challenges instead of viewing them as hindrances is instrumental in reaching success. Keeping a strong attitude and staying optimistic even when faced with adversity keeps your eye on the prize and discourages those self-defeating thoughts. Accomplishments are rarely achieved alone, meaning that the power of your mentality will collaborate with outside help in achieving your goals.

6.Surrounding Yourself with Support

Finding people with the same goals and values who form a part of your support system is essential to advancing on the path to success. Your social network can be very helpful for gaining inspiration and encouragement. While some may cast doubts upon your abilities, others will offer unwavering support and guidance. Be open to advice and stay humble; personal growth is the key to reaching your objectives. However, always remember that your journey is unique, and while advice is invaluable, the final decision must always be your own.

7.Ethical Pursuit of Success

Success should not be achieved if it means disregarding ethics and integrity. Your standards should act as your guide and not be discarded as you strive to attain success. Remain faithful to your principles and make sure you meet the expectations that you have for yourself and the ones other people have of you. The allure of shortcuts and unethical means may be tempting, but the cost is often far greater than any benefit. Success achieved through dishonesty or unethical practices is fragile and unsustainable, often leading to negative consequences in the long run.

8.Expressing Gratitude

As you move forward on your journey to success, it is important to recognize and show gratitude to all those who have aided you on the way. No one is able to attain success single-handedly; it is the result of a number of people coming together and helping one another. Show appreciation for their contributions, and keep these positive influences close. Building a competent team, a support system, is not just advisable; it's essential. Collective effort enhances productivity, fosters innovation, and is instrumental in helping you achieve your goals.

9.Working Together for a Better World

Remember that success is not solely about personal accomplishments. Making an effort to do good and cooperate with others has the potential to create a positive effect on our world and the people in it.

Working together ethically can give us a more promising future. As you climb the ladder of success, strive to uplift those around you. Provide those lacking advantages with your skills, insights, and materials. Doing so can make your triumph a symbol of expectation and a motivator for others.

Achieving success is no easy feat; it demands hard work, dedicated devotion, strong moral beliefs, and an outlook of optimism. It is essential to keep in mind that success is not a one-time arrival but rather an ongoing advancement and accomplishment. Therefore, get off on the right foot, put your all into your endeavors, and continually move closer to the life you long for. Bear in mind that success does not exist solely for its own sake; it is a tool to create a better world for all and an improved personal situation for you.

Strategies For Achieving Success

1.Accomplishments

Accomplishments don't occur just once; they're an ongoing process. Strategies for attaining success involve never ceasing to gain knowledge and to alter oneself if needed, persevering even when you fall short, making efficient use of your time and focusing, overcoming the inclination to put off essential tasks, taking care of your physical and mental health, being informed about finances, evaluating and commending your progress, aiding others by tutoring or through charity.

2.Continuous Learning and Adaptation

To be successful, staying the same is not an option. We should be aware of the fluctuation of the world around us and that what was useful one day may not be beneficial the following day.

Therefore, it is necessary to keep learning and researching. We should invest in understanding new skills and tools in our areas of expertise, as well as attending conferences, reading books, and paying attention to recent developments and advancements. Ultimately, our malleability to new situations and creativity sets the very successful apart from the rest.

3.Resilience in the Face of Failure

Failing isn't the termination of the road; it's the start of the next leg of the journey to success. Everyone who has found success has experienced difficulties and bumps in the road. It's not the failure that decides your future; it's how you handle it. See failures as a means to gain knowledge and expand. Remain solid when weathering a challenge, and contemplate each setback as an important educational tool that will bring you nearer to your objectives. Recall that even the most prosperous people got turned down many times before reaching their greatest successes.

4.Time Management and Prioritization

Time is a finite and precious resource. People who achieve their goals recognize the significance of managing their time well and prioritizing their tasks. Develop a timetable that allows enough time to make progress toward your objectives while also ensuring a harmonious balance between your work and personal life. Identify your most important tasks and tackle them first. Avoid the trap of busyness without productivity. Set clear boundaries and learn to say no to tasks and commitments that do not align with your objectives.

5.Overcoming Procrastination

Procrastination is the arch-nemesis of productivity and success. It's the art of delaying important tasks in favor of less critical ones. To overcome procrastination, break your goals into smaller, manageable tasks. This makes the path to success less daunting. Also, try to come up with ways to make tasks more fun or satisfying, which can give you the drive to begin. Keep in mind that beginning is usually the most difficult yet also the most important step.

6.Health and Well-being

Achieving success isn't just about work-related achievements; it's also about being content with one's life. Neglecting your health can hinder your journey to success. Prioritize physical health through regular exercise and a balanced diet. Equally important is mental health. Practice stress management techniques, meditation, or mindfulness to keep your mind sharp and focused. A healthy body and mind are essential tools in your arsenal as you strive for success.

7.Financial Literacy and Planning

It is important to familiarize yourself with the fundamentals of financial knowledge, including budgeting, saving, and investing, in order to achieve success. Draft a financial plan tailored to your future ambitions to help secure economic stability. Avoid unnecessary debt and make informed financial decisions. Remember that financial freedom can provide you with the resources and flexibility to pursue your passions and dreams.

8.Measuring and Celebrating Success

While the journey to success is ongoing, it's essential to pause and celebrate your achievements along the way. Acknowledge your progress and the milestones you've reached. This not only boosts your morale but also provides motivation to continue pushing forward. Celebrating success reinforces the positive habits and behaviors that got you there in the first place.

9.Giving Back and Mentorship

As you move along the path to success, ruminate on the effect you can have on the individuals around you. Mentoring is an influential practice to aid your area and field. Visualize your education and accomplishments when educating the next generation; this benefits them and helps you remember what you've learned. Giving to notable causes and being generous to those in need is an invigorating side of success that helps make the world a better place.

1.Components For Achieving Success

The route to success requires an assemblage of characteristic elements like creating connections, being enterprising and inventive, adapting to different circumstances, being perceptive about people and situations, making sure the operation is steadfast and ethical, forming strength and proactive thinking, recognizing the benefits of failing and keeping an ideal balance among drive and satisfaction. Together, these components make up the essence of a sound, perpetual achievement.

2.Networking and Relationship Building

Establishing and sustaining a robust system of professional connections is key to achieving success. Attend business gatherings, become a member of specialized groups, and seek out people who can offer insightful advice and assistance. This will help open doors to a variety of opportunities, allowing you to gain knowledge from the experiences of others. Remember that success is not a solitary endeavor; it often thrives in the connections you cultivate.

3.Risk-Taking and Innovation

Success rarely comes to those who play it safe at all times. Taking calculated risks is often a necessary step on the path to significant achievement. Welcome fresh concepts and be prepared to investigate unconventional techniques and proposals. Accept that mistakes are a realistic consequence of venturing forth, but they can sometimes result in transformative discoveries or objective data, which is beneficial. Consider the risks intently, but do not let the dread of not succeeding bar you from striving ahead with innovative propositions and openings.

4.Adaptability in a Changing World

The modern landscape is one that moves at great speed, and being able to adjust to new situations is an invaluable aptitude. Industries and markets evolve, and unexpected challenges arise. Successful individuals understand the importance of staying flexible and open to change. Embrace change as an opportunity for growth rather than a threat. Be willing to pivot your strategies, learn new skills, and adapt to shifting circumstances. Those who can adapt thrive in an ever-changing landscape.

5.Emotional Intelligence

Developing one's capability to understand and control one's emotions, in addition to becoming more attuned to the feelings of other individuals, is referred to as emotional intelligence or EQ. This has a significant influence on the quality of interpersonal relationships, management considerations, and choices made. Cultivating emotional intelligence can help refine communication, empathy, and managerial skills, which are beneficial in pursuing success.

6.Sustainability and Social Responsibility

In the modern era, achieving success is closely linked to both the environment and social responsibility. Those who focus on the impact they have on the planet and the people around them are often seen in a more positive light by customers, partners, and society as a whole. It is important to think about the consequences of your actions and decisions and make a conscious effort to select options that benefit both the Earth and the communities you are involved with.

7.Cultivating Resilience

Being resilient means having the strength to overcome difficulties and tough times. It's a quality that can be cultivated and improved with experience. When striving for success, you will inevitably encounter obstacles and periods of uncertainty. Cultivating resilience means developing the mental and emotional fortitude to weather these storms and continue moving forward. Practices like being mindful, taking care of oneself, and seeking advice from people one can rely on can all foster resilience.

8.Creativity and Problem-Solving

Problem-solving helps you come up with suitable solutions to the obstacles you face. Generating creative ideas and seeking solutions to obstacles are two essential components of success. Creativity enables one to think outside the norm, envisage new concepts, and confront hurdles from different viewpoints. Problem-solving equips you with the ability to come up with apt answers to the troubles you are met with. Problem-solving enables you to tackle obstacles systematically and find effective solutions. Develop your imaginative productivity by engaging in activities such as brainstorming, artistic endeavors, or venturing into new adventures. Strengthen your problem-solving capabilities by breaking complicated concerns into simple actions and asking for feedback from those around you.

9.Understanding the Power of Failure

Failure does not have to signify a complete conclusion; it is merely an alternate route to accomplishment. Numerous achievement-oriented persons have experienced difficulties in the past that later resulted in their standout successes. In the event of an unsuccessful outcome, sit down and think about where things went awry for you to benefit from while improving in every other aspect. Think about failure as an instructor, not a sign of dismal capabilities or ability.

10. Balancing Ambition and Well-being

Ambitiousness can be an influential factor in accomplishing accomplishments, but it is important to find a middle ground between your career objectives and looking after your own well-being. If you push yourself too hard and forget to take care of yourself, overexertion could cause fatigue and harm your physical and mental health. Success is not sustainable if it comes at the expense of your well-being. Prioritize self-care, maintain a healthy work-life balance, and know when to rest and recharge.

The road to success is a complex and multifaceted journey guided by a diverse set of principles and skills. It requires a combination of determination, adaptability, emotional intelligence, and a commitment to growth.

Remember that success is not a fixed destination but an ever-evolving process. Embrace the challenges, learn from your experiences, and continue to refine your approach as you pursue your goals and aspirations. Your unique journey to success is a testament to your resilience and the positive impact you can have on your life and the world.

It's worth keeping in mind that our achievements were not solely our own doing. Throughout the journey, there were those who assisted us in attaining our objectives. Such people provided constant backing and motivation and pushed us to be bold enough to follow our dreams. Showing appreciation by recognizing their contributions and expressing gratitude for their participation in our successes is vital.

It is crucial that we maintain the presence of these valued individuals on our path to achievement as a token of our gratitude. Such individuals have positive energy and share our mindset, making them the perfect fit to be on our team. Our journey ahead will bring in more optimists and help us build a remarkable crew that collaborates remarkably to achieve a shared objective.

Forming a competent group is critical to our success. The collective effort enables us to reach our goals and improve our output. It's important to remember that there is no one person above the team, and collaboration is key to accomplishing our tasks. Nonetheless, occasionally, someone may not fit in with the team's flow, and it's essential to separate amicably. Instead of creating issues or animosity, you can inform them that they are on a different trajectory and that splitting up is the best decision for everyone.

Accomplishing success requires the assistance of others, and expressing appreciation toward those who have supported us is important. Working with the appropriate team can enable us to achieve anything we desire. It's important to recall that success is not solely based on personal accomplishments but rather on the constructive influence we have on our environment and society. Therefore, let us work toward victory through ethical practices and unite in making a better world.

Chapter 4: Two Doors Close; Go Through the Window

There are countless moments when you'll feel the urge to surrender. Starting afresh may bring numerous instances when you contemplate throwing in the towel. In the midst of all the confusion and apprehension, it is essential to stay linked to the wonder that is your life. Anxiety may overrun your mind occasionally, but recollect not to capitulate. Refrain from giving in, however difficult the situation may be. Persevere, even when it feels like the odds are against you. Understand that a grand plan is unfolding specifically for you, and nothing and no one can snatch that away. What is meant for you will always find its way.

It's imperative to hold onto your faith. Countless challenges in this world can easily lead you to abandon your dreams. Numerous sleepless nights have brought tears streaming down my face. The weight of those nights made it impossible to find rest, robbing me of sleep and peace of mind. The days seemed unbearable, almost pushing me to the brink of insanity.

Your mind is a precious organ that must be guarded at all costs. When obstacles arise, and even when specific individuals become obstacles themselves, remember that some people can be your worst enemies, depending on who they are. But when others start talking, don't fret. Their words suggest that you are on the path to success. Once you reach the pinnacle of success, be prepared to become the topic of conversation. As you surpass others and achieve greatness, you become a headline, capturing attention and admiration. Accept that your accomplishments will motivate others, and you will be a role model and an object of envy for people who wish to take the same path as you.

Despite the highs and lows, proceed onward. Do not allow hesitation, reservations, or hindrances to deviate you from your journey. Trust in the journey and the destination that awaits. Even when some try to make you doubt yourself, you have the potential to achieve remarkable feats.

Remember, there will always be moments when giving up seems tempting but resist that urge. Stay connected to your dreams, stay resilient, and keep moving forward. Your perseverance will guide you to the extraordinary life meant for you.

The reason people may talk behind your back is often because you're already ahead of them. When you're making progress and achieving success, it can breed envy and insecurity in others. Instead of celebrating your accomplishments, they resort to gossip and negativity.

Empathy, on the other hand, is a powerful force. It has the ability to spread and influence those around us. When we show genuine concern and understanding for others, it can create a ripple effect of compassion. Unfortunately, not everyone possesses this quality. Some individuals need more interest, patience, and passion. They need to be more motivated and interested in making something out of their lives. As a result, they don't want others to succeed either.

These people resemble crabs in a barrel, constantly trying to pull you down to keep you at their level. Beware, for these individuals 0can be dangerous. They have nothing to lose and will go to great lengths to demolish your goals. It's similar to the saying my mother used to share, "people like that will cut their noses off to spite their face." They will try to make your journey difficult and close every door.

However, it's important to remember that it's not your battle to fight. It's not your mission to prove yourself to these individuals. Instead, you must swiftly remove yourself from their negativity, take stock of your surroundings, and quickly pivot to another door. Redirect your focus and center yourself on the opportunities that lie ahead.

Moving swiftly and decisively is critical. Don't allow their toxic behavior to hinder your progress or dampen your spirit. Keep pushing forward, embracing your own unique path. Surround yourself with supportive and uplifting individuals who genuinely want to see you succeed.

The reason some people talk behind your back is often rooted in their own insecurities and envy. However, don't let their negativity deter you from pursuing your goals. Empathy can be contagious, and it's essential to cultivate it within yourself. Stay focused, remove yourself from toxic influences, and continue forging on your remarkable journey.

My mother always said that time is just as important as money, and it's not wise to squander it. With a plan, it's possible to make progress or accomplish ambitions. Every moment is priceless, so it's essential to keep focused and not lose a single second. Sometimes, you may feel the minutes are running away, and there's no chance of miscalculating. Still, remain confident in yourself even amidst obstacles. Believe that you can survive any obstacle you face. It's all right if you eventually choose a different approach. By altering your position, adjusting your activities, and taking an alternative approach, you may have more chances to better yourself.

Sometimes, you may lose your footing and fall, but don't give up. Pick yourself up and keep going. It's all part of the process. Be confident and never give up; that will be the driving force that will get you to your destination. Believe in yourself and your talents, as they will sustain you.

If, at first, you don't succeed, it's crucial to rise again. Restart, regroup, and be willing to knock on another door. Persistence pays off, and someone, somewhere, will recognize your worth and grant you the opportunity you seek. Even if you must explore unconventional routes or take risks through a metaphorical window, seize any opening.

Understanding that greatness doesn't require perfection from the start is essential. You don't have to be flawless or extraordinary right away. But you must take that first step, no matter how small, to embark on the journey toward greatness. Move forward, inch by inch, and don't let setbacks discourage you. When one door closes, another will inevitably open, revealing new possibilities and chances for success. In your pursuit of your goals, never give up. Giving in, accepting defeat, or settling for less are not options in your vocabulary. Banish the words "enough," "no," "maybe," and "if" from your mindset. Embrace resilience, determination, and unwavering belief in yourself. Your dedication and steadfast focus will propel you toward achieving greatness. The clock is ticking, so make every second count.

Success is a challenging journey. It requires unwavering determination and an unyielding spirit. Within your vocabulary lies the phrase "I will make it through thick and thin, through whatever it takes." This mindset encapsulates your refusal to give up, no matter how long it may take. With this mindset, you move swiftly and quickly toward your goals, knowing that giving up is not an option.

Obstacles may appear in your path, but you see them for what they are: mere hurdles to overcome. They hold no power to deter you, for you understand that obstacles are simply part of the journey. Similarly, people are just individuals; their opinions or actions do not sway your determination. You move quietly, avoiding unnecessary distractions, and continue on your path with unwavering focus.

As you forge ahead, you surpass every obstacle and leave behind those who doubted you. Before they realize it, you will have already reached your destination. Your quiet determination and swift progress will leave them astounded. You achieve your goals not through shortcuts or unethical means but by doing things correctly. You seize opportunities and make the most of them, always moving in the right direction. You understand that success is not confined to a singular aspect of life. It encompasses your career, your personal growth, and your overall fulfillment. To reach this success, you never allow anyone or anything to hinder your progress. No external force can derail your journey because you possess the determination and resilience to overcome any obstacle.

The essence of success lies within this mindset and approach. It is the unwavering belief that you will make it through any circumstance. It is the ability to persevere, adapt, and overcome challenges that arise. Your commitment to never giving up and always moving forward defines your path to success.

One should stay focused in life and let nothing stand in the way when facing challenges. Moving swiftly and quietly can help to triumph over any obstacle or adversity, and success awaits those who refuse to be deterred. This is the mindset that the speaker has always maintained throughout their journey. Successful people have an agenda, a unique journey, and powerful testimony. It has never been easy for me, as I have endured immense hardships and persevered through the storm.

The one thing I constantly reminded myself of was that "no" was never an option. I kept pushing forward, refusing to accept defeat. I understood that simply trying was not always enough to achieve success. It required certain essential elements, which I refer to as PDH: Passion,

Determination, and Humbleness, symbolized by the initials of my name, Pamela D. Hogan. Passion is a vital component of success. It fuels the drive to keep moving forward. Regardless of the obstacles or people that may try to hinder your progress, passion empowers you to overcome them. It resides deep within your soul and becomes a constant source of motivation. When you possess the passion, nothing and no one can strip it away from you.

Passion transcends the importance of money. It becomes a way of life, a source of joy and fulfillment. It drives you to excel and achieve greatness. With passion, you derive immense satisfaction from your pursuits, and it becomes a driving force behind your actions and decisions.

However, passion alone is not enough. Determination is another crucial element in the path to success. It is the unwavering commitment to your goals and the relentless pursuit of excellence. Determination pushes you to go the extra mile and to keep striving when others may give up. It helps you weather the storms and overcome the hurdles that come your way.

Humbleness, the third pillar of success, keeps you grounded and open to growth. You can grow and improve by incorporating input from those around you. Humility gives you the attitude to appreciate the successes that come your way while remaining humble and thankful for your experiences. My ambition to advance has been a driving force in my professional life, allowing me to persevere and revel in my triumphs, big or small. Developing a composed attitude toward hardships has encouraged me to remain focused and strive to achieve my goals. My commitment to excellence, along with my humble outlook, has been the guide that has led me to success. Passion ignites the fire within, determination fuels perseverance, and humbleness keeps us grounded on our journey. With these qualities, we can navigate any challenge and achieve our goals, finding true fulfillment.

The saying goes, “When you have a job you love, you’ll never work a day in your life.” This simple yet profound statement holds a great truth. It all comes down to passion. When you possess a genuine passion for something, it ceases to feel like work. It becomes a labor of love, an endeavor that fills your heart and soul.

When you dedicate yourself to something you are passionate about, you will find joy in the process of helping others and seeing success. This applies to goals and career paths, as having a personal connection will drive your devotion.

Reaching success is generally not a simple experience. You require immense passion and conviction for it. No matter what difficulties you go through, you need to commit and persist. Maintaining an unwavering faith that this is what your destiny is meant to be is crucial. No amount of negativity or closed doors should deter you. Instead, focus on the positive, keep moving forward, and remain determined. Sometimes, the road may seem blocked, but that should never discourage you. When a door closes, be willing to find an alternative route. Adaptability and perseverance are key. If necessary, be prepared to go through the window and take unconventional paths in pursuit of your dreams. But always remember to do it in the right way, with integrity and respect.

The true meaning is found in this combination of passion and determination. It is the willingness to face challenges head-on, overcome obstacles, and maintain a sense of purpose. When you have the drive to push through any adversity, you will not only achieve your goals but also find fulfillment along the way.

Take hold of your enthusiasm, chase after your objectives, and let persistence be your powerhouse. The labor you do will no longer be like work but instead a reflection of your innermost hopes. With every ounce of strength you have, commit yourself to it, and you will construct an existence that is not only full of purpose but also brimming with pleasure and satisfaction.

Underlining the significance of humility, the text stresses that it is a key factor in achieving prosperity. Keeping one's head down and realizing the assistance from other folks that made it possible to reach one's goals is vital. No matter how much success has been achieved, it is necessary to remember not to feel superior to others and keep a willingness to listen and learn from them.

You acknowledge that you are in a constant state of learning. Age and wealth do not exempt you from the process. No matter how old or rich you become, you remain open to new knowledge and insights from others. You understand there is always something to gain from someone else's experiences. Remaining humble is an essential part of your daily learning. You embrace the notion of surrendering to what is good for you and being open to new opportunities for growth. Humility enables you to recognize when it is necessary to step back, accept guidance, and learn from others. By humbling yourself when needed, you pave the way for further success.

In this mindset, you will continue to succeed. By including meekness in your day-to-day activities, you cultivate an atmosphere suitable for personal and professional development. You remind yourself that succeeding does not entitle you to look down on others; rather, it is an indication of your determination to learn, adjust, and stay the course. Through humbleness, you preserve a flexible mindset, prepared to take in new ideas and information that will advance your progress.

As you march ahead with unwavering determination, remember that humility is your guiding principle. A humble mindset and staying open to learning from others is essential for successful growth and achievement. By embracing humility, one will have the strength and determination to move forward with purpose and reap the rewards of their successes. It serves as a constant reminder of the support and guidance that have shaped your journey thus far. No matter how high you climb the ladder of success, you remain grounded, knowing that seeking assistance and continuously learning are crucial for growth. Humility plays a significant role in keeping you connected to your roots. It reminds you of the people who have contributed to your achievements and encourages you to appreciate their impact. With humility, you embrace the virtue of listening and learning from others, recognizing that no amount of wealth or accomplishments should ever make you consider yourself as being better than anyone else.

You strongly think that gaining knowledge is an activity that never ends regardless of age or financial wealth. You are aware that wisdom can come from unexpected sources, and everyone has something to contribute. Keeping an open mind to new information and ideas from other people allows you to experience the world from multiple perspectives and heightens your comprehension.

Maintaining a humble mindset is essential to your daily pursuit of knowledge. You willingly surrender to what is good for your personal and professional growth, even if it means stepping back and seeking guidance from others. By humbling yourself when necessary, you create opportunities for learning and set the stage for further success.

By utilizing humility, one can achieve personal and professional growth. Success is not a sign of superiority but rather a sign of dedication to learning, adapting, and persevering. It is essential to remain humble and open-minded to new ideas that can promote further success. Let's delve further into the concept of time, the importance of adaptability, and the enduring value of humility:

Time as a Precious Resource:

Time, often overlooked and underestimated, is the most precious resource we possess. It's the one resource that, once spent, can never be replenished or regained. In a world that constantly demands our attention and offers endless distractions, understanding and harnessing the power of time becomes imperative for achieving success.

Successful individuals have a profound respect for time. They recognize that it's not just something that passes by; it's a currency they can invest wisely or squander recklessly. This perspective drives them to set clear priorities and establish well-structured schedules. They grasp that time is finite, and to optimize it, they must assign it to the matters that hold the utmost importance.

One of the prime foes of achievement is procrastination. It sneaks in surreptitiously, frequently masquerading as a harmless delay, and before one realizes it, it has filched valuable hours, days, or even years from one's existence. Procrastination is the silent assassin of dreams and ambitions, and it thrives in the absence of discipline and effective time management.

To combat procrastination and unlock the true potential of time, one must cultivate discipline and sharpen their time-management skills. Discipline forms the bedrock of success; it's the aptitude to execute what must be executed, even when the inclination to do so is absent. Discipline empowers you to withstand the allure of procrastination and stay resolute on your objectives. Efficient time management is the craft of optimizing your daily routines and tasks to boost productivity. It encompasses planning, structuring, and prioritizing your engagements. It signifies establishing specific goals and breaking them down into attainable phases. It's about creating a roadmap for your day and following it diligently.

A formidable time-management tactic is the Eisenhower Matrix, which categorizes tasks into four segments contingent on their urgency and significance. This matrix aids you in pinpointing what demands instant attention, what can be scheduled for later, what can be delegated, and what can be excluded. By employing this method, you can confirm that you devote your time to tasks that genuinely hold value.

Another critical aspect of effective time management is the minimization of distractions. In today's digital era, distractions are everywhere, from social media alerts to the incessant chime of emails. These disruptions can derail your concentration and steal precious minutes from your day. Flourishing individuals excel at overseeing these interruptions by defining limits, using productivity apps, and engaging in mindfulness.

Additionally, time management isn't solely about being preoccupied; it's about being productive. Many individuals equate a congested timetable with efficiency, but often, it's the reverse. Success emanates from executing the appropriate tasks efficiently, not from merely executing more. Consequently, it's pivotal to recognize your most crucial tasks and focus on dedicating your time and effort to them. It's also essential to comprehend that time management is a dynamic procedure. Your priorities and aspirations can change, and external variables can impact your timetable.

Flexibility is key. Successful individuals adapt to changing circumstances while maintaining a focus on their long-term objectives.

Furthermore, delegation is a priceless aptitude in time management. You can't carry out everything solo, and striving to do so will only lead to exhaustion. Successful individuals grasp their strengths and weaknesses and assign tasks that others can carry out more proficiently. This not only liberates their time but also ascertains that tasks are executed effectively.

Time stands as the most valuable resource in our possession, and the manner in which we handle it significantly influences our achievement and contentment in life. Successful individuals understand this and approach time management with discipline, organization, and a clear sense of priorities. They recognize that procrastination is the enemy of progress and that distractions must be managed. They adapt to changing circumstances and delegate tasks wisely. Ultimately, they make every moment count in their journey toward success.

Adaptability and the Art of Pivoting:

Adaptability is a quality that has gained substantial importance in our rapidly changing universe. In today's dynamic and capricious setting, triumph is not merely the outcome of adhering to a rigid plan or pursuing an unalterable set of actions. Instead, it depends on one's capacity to adapt and pivot when circumstances alter.

At its essence, adaptability pertains to the readiness and competence to amend one's strategy or tactic when the current route no longer advances the desired result. It's the recognition that what functioned yesterday may not be effective tomorrow and the willingness to navigate unexplored territory when necessary.

Consider a business proprietor who, for numerous years, depended on conventional in-person sales. With the emergence of online commerce and shifting consumer inclinations, foot traffic to the physical shop dwindled. In this situation, adaptability becomes the lifeline. The proprietor must be open to the concept of altering their business model, investing in an online presence, and learning the fundamentals of digital marketing. By accepting these changes and adapting to the changing landscape, they possess the prospect to endure and flourish.

Adaptability also extends to personal and professional growth. As individuals, we set goals and plan our career trajectories. However, life often throws curveballs, such as unexpected job loss, shifts in industries, or economic downturns. Those who possess adaptability are better equipped to weather such storms. Instead of clutching to a declining enterprise, they are more prone to map out a fresh course, acquire novel skills, or explore alternative career paths.

The concept of adaptability is tightly connected to the notion that success isn't a fixed destination but an incessantly evolving expedition. Those who view success as a destination often find themselves stuck when circumstances change. They may become rigid and resistant to change, believing their established methods will always lead to victory. Regrettably, this outlook can result in stagnation and ultimate downfall.

On the contrary, individuals who apprehend that success is a journey are more inclined to embrace adaptability as a pivotal instrument. They view each predicament as a chance to gain knowledge, evolve, and pivot if required. This adaptability in approach empowers them to remain pertinent, inventive, and resilient when confronted with adversity.

Adjusting to change is not invariably effortless. It necessitates a specific level of humility to concede that the current path isn't yielding the preferred outcomes. It demands courage to step into the unknown and take calculated risks. It necessitates continuous learning and a willingness to let go of old habits and mindsets.

In the business world, iconic examples of adaptability abound. Consider the transformation of Nokia, a company once synonymous with mobile phones. When the smartphone revolution disrupted the mobile industry, Nokia initially struggled to adapt. However, the company eventually recognized the need for a radical shift in strategy. They pivoted toward network infrastructure and telecommunications, a move that saved the company from obsolescence.

Similarly, the COVID-19 pandemic forced numerous businesses to pivot or perish. Restaurants turned to takeout and delivery, schools shifted to remote learning, and many companies adopted telecommuting. Those who adapted swiftly to the new circumstances survived, while those resistant to change faced dire consequences.

Originality and adaptability are often interwoven. When individuals or organizations agree to experiment with fresh approaches, test innovative technologies, and explore varied paths, they situate themselves to seize fresh prospects. This is rampant in the technology sector, where corporations such as Apple continually overhaul their products and services to stay ahead of the competition.

Collaboration is another aspect of adaptability. In a world where knowledge and expertise are distributed across diverse individuals and groups, collaborating with others can be a powerful way to adapt and thrive. One can overcome challenges and tap into new markets or audiences by seeking partnerships and working with individuals with complementary skills and perspectives.

The Everlasting Value of Humility:

Humility, often regarded as a simple virtue, holds profound significance in the journey of personal and professional growth. It functions as the foundation of authentic success, serving as a reminder that our accomplishments don't solely stem from our individual exertions but rather originate from cooperation, backing, and the lessons absorbed from others.

At its essence, humility is about acknowledging that we aren't isolated in our pursuits. Regardless of how competent, skilled, or intelligent we may be, our journey to success is intertwined with the contributions of countless individuals. It involves recognizing the mentors who guided us, the comrades who toiled alongside us, and even the rivals who propelled us to enhance. In doing so, we not only pay tribute to those who have played a part in our voyage but also gain a more profound reverence for the subtleties of accomplishment.

Crucially, humility doesn't belittle one's triumphs; it enhances them. When we unreservedly acknowledge the backing and direction we've received along the path, it lends authenticity to our success. Instead of being viewed as mere achievements, our accomplishments become the result of a collective effort, a testimony to the strength of collaboration. This acknowledgment, in turn, encourages a spirit of appreciation. Gratitude holds substantial sway. It reminds us of the privilege and responsibility that accompany success. It compels us to give back, to support and mentor others as we were supported and mentored. Humility, then, becomes a catalyst for a cycle of positive impact. Those who have benefited from the wisdom and generosity of others feel compelled to pass it on, creating a ripple effect that extends far beyond individual achievements.

Furthermore, humility prompts us to remain open to learning throughout our lives. Irrespective of how much expertise we accumulate, there is perpetually room to augment our knowledge and broaden our viewpoints. The realization that others possess valuable insights to offer, regardless of their background or experience, keeps us modest and inquisitive.

In a society that frequently praises self-assuredness and the façade of infallibility, humility offers a refreshing counterbalance. It permits us to concede when we lack knowledge and to seek guidance without fearing judgment. This willingness to learn sustains intellectual engagement and enables personal development.

One of the most profound facets of humility is its ability to engender empathy. When we recognize that our success doesn't solely hinge on our own endeavors, we become more receptive to the trials and tribulations encountered by others. We sympathize with those who are still navigating their path to success, cognizant that we, too, were once in their shoes.

Humility also plays a crucial role in leadership. Leaders who are humble are more approachable and relatable to their teams. They are open to listening, learning, and admitting their errors, fostering an atmosphere where others feel at ease doing the same. In such a climate, innovation and progress flourish, as individuals aren't hesitant to express their ideas and concerns.

Moreover, humble leaders tend to attract and retain top talent. Employees are more likely to respect leaders who don't flaunt their achievements but instead concentrate on the collective accomplishments of the team. This, in turn, leads to a more engaged and motivated workforce.

In the grand mosaic of human history, humility has been a recurring theme among some of the most exceptional individuals. Figures like Mahatma Gandhi, Mother Teresa, and Nelson Mandela are lauded not only for their achievements but also for their profound humility. They understood that their work was part of a larger movement and remained humble in the face of adversity and success.

Humility is not a fleeting virtue; it endures. It is a quality that not only enhances our personal and professional achievements but also enriches our lives and the lives of those around us. It reminds us that success is a shared journey, that gratitude and learning are lifelong companions, and that empathy and humility are the cornerstones of a more compassionate and interconnected world. This recognition fosters a spirit of cooperation and unity that transcends individual accomplishments and creates a better world for all. In a world often marked by ego and self-promotion, humility is a timeless value that continues to shine brightly. Incorporating these principles – effective time management, adaptability, and humility – into your pursuit of success enriches your journey and enhances your chances of achieving not just success but lasting fulfillment. These values are not mere concepts but actionable steps that can propel you forward on your remarkable path.

As you forge ahead with unwavering determination, always remember that humility is your guiding principle. No matter how much one may achieve, it's important to have a humble mindset and acknowledge that one is just a fraction of something larger. Lessons and experiences should be embraced with an open mind, attentive listening, and adaptation. Incorporating humility in one's journey can lead to thriving and achieving great things. Winning the lottery may seem like an overnight success, but it's not a one-time event and doesn't happen suddenly. The lottery functions differently, presenting both fortunate and unfortunate aspects.

Realizing success isn't easy; it necessitates a lot of effort and commitment. While it might be nice to have accomplishments come without any effort, it's the journey that is vital. When you invest your vitality, exertion, and devotion into something, your admiration of it elevates to a greater level. You treasure it, hold it dear, and go that additional mile to sustain it.

This lesson holds significant importance in life. Understanding what is truly valuable and being willing to protect it at all costs is an invaluable virtue. This transcends tangible possessions and extends to connections, personal development, and the things that genuinely bring contentment. When you acknowledge the significance of something, you organically foster a sense of duty toward it. Moreover, part of this responsibility lies in helping others who are deserving and share a similar mindset. Just as someone once helped you, you have the opportunity to pay it forward. You encounter individuals who possess the same determination, passion, and willingness to make sacrifices. They may just need a helping hand to ascend the ladder of success.

By extending your support to those who are like-minded and have the potential to achieve greatness, you contribute to their journey. You can reach down and uplift them, providing the guidance and assistance they need to move forward. In accomplishing this, you initiate a ripple effect of empowerment and advancement.

This ripple effect of empowerment and growth bears witness to the influence of communal knowledge and backing. As you progress on your path to triumph, bear in mind that you're not isolated. Just as others have supported you in your pursuit, be prepared to extend a helping hand to those who exhibit the same determination and enthusiasm.

Success is not an individual pursuit; it's a collective endeavor. When you invest in the development and triumph of others, you fortify the bonds of your community and construct a network of kindred individuals who can elevate each other. This sensation of camaraderie and mutual encouragement evolves into a wellspring of inspiration and motivation, propelling everyone involved to attain even their more challenging goals. In addition to aiding others, it's imperative to stay adaptable and receptive to fresh prospects. Flexibility and the readiness to explore uncharted territory can result in remarkable breakthroughs. Furthermore, as you continue on your journey, always bear in mind the value of time. Time is a finite resource, and every instant matters. Employ your time carefully, concentrating on undertakings and pursuits that align with your objectives and principles. Abstain from procrastination and distractions that can obstruct your advancement. Pledge to make the most of each day, inching closer to your aspirations.

In conclusion, your course to success depends upon ardor, determination, modesty, and a pledge to help others along the way. It's about recognizing the significance of what you possess and being conscientious guardians of your success. Remain open to education, adjust to evolving conditions, and optimize your time. In doing so, you will persist in thriving and inspiring others on their journeys toward greatness.

Chapter 5: Boss Up!

You made it! You succeeded, and you should be very proud of yourself. Now, you are the boss you were born to be! By now, I know you are overwhelmed with joy. You went through the storms. You made your sacrifices and achieved your goals. You are right where the universe commanded you to be. You have always had the potential to be a boss, and throughout the various trials and tribulations, you have never wavered in your ultimate goals. Your focus and hard work have paid off, and you have earned the right to revel in the delight of your accomplishment. Every step you took and every decision you made was in service of the realization of your true purpose - to be your own boss. Now, be proud of yourself and continue standing tall as you have arrived at the place you were always meant to be.

It's time to look back and celebrate the risks you took in life that have paid off. You possessed the courage and conviction to put your trust in yourself, even though the results were unknown.

To succeed, you had to be daring and take the chance of a successful outcome. You envisioned success in your life, and you backed it up with actions that created it. Don't forget that your words are powerful, and by openly declaring your ambitions, you bring them into existence. Being in a leadership role means that you must accept that difficulties will come up. It is vital to put in the work and come up with creative ideas to keep your spot at the top. It is important to be ready to face these problems head-on. As a leader, you must stay ahead of the game by welcoming change and being open to fresh perspectives. Remain pliant and adjust to various situations, as this will help you be resilient and cope with the continuous changes and turns encountered in life.

It is essential for you to have effective communication as a leader. Being able to articulate your goals and expectations and generating enthusiasm among your team will make you stand out. Your words have power; thus, you should use them to encourage and embolden those around you.

Gaining the capability to make prudent decisions is imperative for those in authority. Prior to deciding on what to do, it is imperative to grasp the particular circumstances and their attainable outcome. It might be advantageous to seek advice from seasoned clairvoyants and study the data at hand rigorously. Utilizing your intuition and background might permit you to shape sensible outcomes.

Additionally, it's wise to recognize the value of staying informed on current events surrounding your industry and employees. Aiding your own growth involves embracing the concept of learning throughout life. Participate in workshops, read useful literature, arrange meetings with mentors, and make use of any other career-enhancing opportunity available to you.

Reaching a position of leadership is a great accomplishment that is not within reach for many. It requires unique qualities such as zeal, conviction, and humility. You have shown yourself to be different, having driven your success through determination, tolerance, and tenacity. All along, you have kept in mind how you need to keep a balance to get where you are today.

Being willing to make compromises is a crucial part of the process, and your understanding of its importance is necessary.

I have clear memories of the many compromises and risks I had to take, even when it meant sacrificing for my own family. That memory still troubles me, and I constantly apologize to our son for the choices I had to make to give both of us a better life. My family also had to make concessions, and I will always be thankful to my husband for caring for our son when I couldn't. Despite being tired from working overnight, he would come home with only a few hours of sleep and ensure that our son was taken care of after getting off the school bus.

Late nights at the salon or travels worldwide to pursue my dream as an international educator required sacrifices from all of us. This is one of many stories I share; one day, you will share your story, too. Your determination is remarkable, having shown its strength through the numerous compromises you have made to move closer to your goals. Your willingness to go through extreme effort and dedication proves your aspirations and objectives are truly dear to you. This unwavering dedication is something to be admired, revealing the immense passion and ambition within you that is leading you toward success. As a leader, your qualities and beliefs have come to symbolize what it takes to be truly great. Your enthusiasm spreads, encouraging others to do their best. Your determination is unwavering and helps everyone get through difficult circumstances. In spite of all of your success, you stay humble, knowing that there are many people who have helped you achieve what you have.

A leader is more than somebody with authority or influence; they create a space that allows people to grow and express themselves in order to reach their highest potential.

Your experiences have given you the knowledge and understanding needed to mentor and instruct those around you, passing on the lessons you have learned. You know the importance of motivating and encouraging your team, understanding that true success comes from everyone doing well.

You possess the necessary characteristics of a leader, which you have showcased with your passion, decisiveness, and modest attitude. Through compromise and overcoming obstacles, you have proven yourself as a successful leader. Your journey has demonstrated that anything is achievable with focus and enthusiasm.

Once you recognize you have the power and self-assurance to rise above any complications and take on life struggles bravely, you can keep progressing. It is significant to recognize that although you trust in a superior existence and recognize God holds the supreme power, you still remain the most significant being in your existence. Honoring and preserving your health is imperative to guarantee that you will always be there to support your beloved family, whom you value greatly. You appreciate the blessing of your family but also recognize that evolving into the best version of yourself is critical to both yourself and your family. You comprehend your value and the importance of your goals, ambitions, and success, all of which you pursue with the purpose of creating a better future for yourself and those around you.

You have done a fantastic job so far. You followed your dreams, struggled to survive, and exerted a lot of effort to attain success. Most importantly, you did all of this for yourself, showing that you are capable, deserving, and can be triumphant. Now, you have to focus on sustaining what you have achieved. The road ahead will take commitment, consistency, and a lot of sacrifices, but you must remember that this is a product of your hard work - you ought to shield it no matter what.

From the start, you will be full of enthusiasm and anticipation to show off your hard work to the world and begin this journey. Nonetheless, once a few weeks pass, you may feel overwhelmed by the obligations necessary to sustain and look after your work.

At times like these, taking a break and inhaling deeply is essential. Bear in mind that this isn't a disaster, even if it may look like one. Anxiety and intensity are all part of the journey you have initiated. Remember the ambitions and aspirations that motivated your mission thus far, along with the sacrifices you have made to get to this point. Don't forget Rome wasn't built in a single day, and your mission requires patience, hard work, and time. Find comfort in the realization that it's all right to take a break and gather yourself. Breathe deeply, and trust that you have the capability to overcome any obstacles in your path. Reflect on the strength and motivation that have aided you thus far. Accept your journey with all its highs and lows; these are all helping you reach your ultimate triumph.

Realizing your worth and taking care of your health and well-being is needed for progress and to be able to provide for others. Your ambitions have gotten you to this place; now it is time to nurture it. Even when times of stress are too much to handle, remember to relax, consider what has happened so far, and be aware that you will make it through anything that arises with lots of hard work, patience, and time. You have already achieved a lot - remain focused and have faith in yourself.

In our busy and ever-changing lives, acquiring points of peace and privacy is fundamental. Setting aside time to concentrate and recenter ourselves can initiate our basic coping impulses and permit us to face our problems. By releasing our minds from the bonds of powerful feelings, we make room for the ability to think clearly and discover solutions.

It is essential to have faith in our individual intellect. Have confidence that you have the skill to maneuver through troublesome scenarios. It might take a while to unravel a problem; however, it is essential to keep in mind that you can ask for support when needed. Locate a peaceful spot in which you can pay attention and focus and visualize the matter as if it were a jigsaw puzzle, breaking it into workable components and carefully forming a response.

Examining each part of a complicated puzzle in isolation should be done. Completing complicated puzzles often necessitates putting in numerous hours of labor over an extended period. When we take a moment to be still and quiet, though, we recognize doors previously undiscovered. Unexpected changes and different outlooks are now visible, making it possible for us to discover the source of the problem and potential answers.

When we recognize the value of time in comparison to money, it is not sensible to waste it. Consequently, we look at the advantages and drawbacks of the options available to us and bring them together in a unified way. After doing this, it is critical that we take action quickly.

Upon resolving our issues, a feeling of relief overtakes us, allowing us to breathe freely once more. It's crucial to keep in mind that we play a significant role in finding solutions. Like tending to a baby, we must also prioritize self-care and nourishment. Granting ourselves a much-needed respite is not just permissible but also essential. If possible, contemplate indulging in a vacation. Alternatively, seek solace in a serene nook of your own garden, transforming it into a personal sanctuary. Rest becomes vital in revitalizing the mind, body, and spirit. Seeking solitude and concentrating on our emotions allows our natural defenses to kick in. We can promote our capabilities and accept that any difficulty can be conquered with the assistance of others and with the passing of time. Seeing issues as challenges and attempting to fix them piece by piece leads to creative solutions. It is vital to act quickly since we are limited in how much time we have. When our problems are resolved, looking after ourselves must be considered a priority. Focusing on self-improvement and creating a peaceful atmosphere are two crucial elements for good health. So, give a warm welcome to the calmness, be confident in your skills, and permit your mind to direct you through the complicated issues that life has in store.

It's a voyage of revelation that entails consistently learning and developing personally. To be successful in this venture, you need command and strategic concepts, as well as a clear-cut direction. Struggles will come your way, but with courage and stamina, you can transcend them and realize your complete effectiveness. Being a leader does not just involve having power; it's more about stimulating and enabling others to excel.

Gaining thorough knowledge of yourself is key to becoming a successful boss. It involves recognizing your talents, strengths, and weaknesses to make informed decisions and fully utilize your capabilities. Understanding your values, ambitions, and motivations contributes to forming a genuine, inspiring leadership approach. With self-awareness comes the acceptance of feedback and opportunities for growth, enabling you to work toward continual self-improvement and advance your career. It is of the utmost importance for a successful boss to have strong communication capabilities. Constructive dialogue is the basis of management, granting you the ability to explain your objectives, give direction, and make valuable connections with your personnel. Open communication promotes openness and discernment, diminishing confusion and establishing reliance and admiration. Being a leader necessitates being an attentive listener, compassionate, and willing to talk, promoting an atmosphere of communication. You can inspire and involve your team by developing your communication skills and cultivating a united and productive work environment.

It is imperative for any leader to have a robust leadership style and decision-making skills. These abilities do not revolve around exact control of the task; instead, they focus on what is required to help the team succeed. Skilled bosses motivate their peers, define objectives, and supply the needed resources to make good progress. Furthermore, making accurate decisions in difficult situations and taking advantage of available prospects is a primary requirement for leaders. To make successful decisions, a leader must be able to assemble essential data, examine it accurately, and make wise calls in agreement with the goal and action plan of the organization.

In order to succeed as a leader, you must be competent, flexible, and strong. The business environment continually changes, so it is necessary to adjust accordingly in order to remain successful in the long run. Changes can range from technological advances to market shifts, so you should be open-minded and able to explore ideas outside of your comfort zone. Additionally, having the capability to recover from difficulties and challenges is key to achieving success. Despite the obstacles that will arise, it is paramount to stay positive and learn from mistakes.

In order to be the most successful boss possible, you need a powerful drive and a clear direction. Your purpose is the flame that leads you and your workforce, no matter how hard the circumstances are. Your vision is the roadmap that shows the end goal and the methods to get there. This composition aids in motivating everybody and helps them stay focused. By constantly reiterating these two things, a sense of unity is produced within the company, along with dedication.

At the end of the day, becoming a top-notch leader is a never-ending process. Essential talents for this path include self-awareness, effective communication, strong management, flexibility, the capacity to recover, and a stated vision and mission. Developing these abilities can help you serve as an inspiration and source of encouragement for others, boosting your team and firm toward success. Leadership is not about having control; it's all about creating a meaningful consequence, bringing out the greatest in those around you, and leaving a lasting legacy. Take up the challenges, take advantage of opportunities, and be the leader you were meant to be.

The Evolution of Leadership

The progression of leadership is an ever-changing process that adjusts to the shifting landscape of the world we inhabit. In earlier times, leadership frequently appeared as a hierarchical approach, with one individual at the helm making choices for the entire group. Nevertheless, as we've moved forward into the contemporary era, leadership has undergone a substantial transformation.

One of the crucial shifts in leadership has been toward a more cooperative and encompassing style. Rather than relying solely on one person's insight, effective leaders of today acknowledge the significance of varied perspectives. They foster open dialogue and embrace input from team members with diverse backgrounds, experiences, and viewpoints. This all-encompassing approach results in improved decision-making and cultivates a sense of belonging among team members, as everyone feels heard and valued.

Another significant factor driving the evolution of leadership is the advent of remote work and digital communication. With the ascent of technology, numerous teams are no longer bound to a physical office space. The capacity to lead in this virtual environment is an indispensable skill for modern leaders.

Leaders now find themselves overseeing virtual teams spread across different locations and time zones. This presents new challenges, including the need for effective remote communication and motivation strategies. Leaders in this digital age must master the art of building connections and a sense of belonging among remote team members. This involves using digital tools and platforms to facilitate meaningful interactions, as well as finding creative ways to maintain team cohesion despite physical distance.

Leadership remains a dynamic concept that evolves in response to changes in technology, culture, and society. Contemporary leaders recognize the significance of inclusivity, collaboration, and adapting to the challenges of remote work. By embracing these changes and continuously developing their skills, leaders can navigate the evolving landscape of leadership successfully.

The Role of Emotional Intelligence

Emotional intelligence (EI) has garnered substantial prominence in the realm of leadership and management, reshaping our perception of effective leadership. This notion centers on the ability to not only perceive but also comprehend and regulate one's emotions, as well as those of others. It's not solely about emotional awareness; it's about utilizing emotions as a valuable instrument for successful leadership.

Leaders with a high degree of emotional intelligence possess a unique set of abilities that set them apart in their roles. Initially, they excel in constructing and preserving robust interpersonal relationships. They have the aptitude to connect with individuals on a profound level, fostering trust and rapport. This relational facet of leadership is paramount, as it paves the way for effective communication and collaboration within a team or organization. Conflict resolution is another area where emotional intelligence shines. Leaders with EI can navigate through disputes with finesse. They can identify the root causes of conflicts, address the emotions involved, and facilitate productive discussions. This prevents conflicts from escalating and transforms them into opportunities for growth and innovation.

Furthermore, leaders with high EI are adept at inspiring and motivating their teams. They possess a sharp understanding of their team members' emotional states and can customize their leadership approach accordingly. This personalized approach resonates with employees, engendering a sense of being valued and understood, which, in turn, boosts morale and productivity.

Empathy, a central component of emotional intelligence, plays a pivotal role in leadership. Leaders who can put themselves in their employees' shoes are better equipped to address concerns and challenges effectively. They provide the necessary support and encouragement, ultimately cultivating a culture of trust and loyalty within the organization.

Continuous development of emotional intelligence is not just a valuable skill for leaders; it's a necessity. As leaders sharpen their EI, they become more adaptable and resilient in the face of change and adversity. They can navigate complex and uncertain situations with grace, making informed decisions that benefit their teams and organizations. Emotional intelligence is no longer a mere soft skill but a cornerstone of effective leadership. Leaders who prioritize the cultivation of emotional intelligence are better positioned to create thriving work environments, resolve conflicts, and inspire their teams to achieve remarkable results.

It's not just about understanding emotions; it's about harnessing them to lead with authenticity, empathy, and effectiveness.

Navigating Challenges and Adversity

No leadership journey is without its share of challenges and adversity. In fact, it's often during these difficult times that leaders are truly tested. How you respond to adversity can define your leadership legacy.

Resilience is a pivotal trait for leaders confronting challenges. It entails the ability to rebound from setbacks and maintain a positive attitude. Resilient leaders inspire their teams to persevere through tough times, knowing that setbacks are opportunities for growth and learning.

Furthermore, adaptability is critical in the swiftly changing world of today. Leaders must be open to change and able to pivot their strategies when required. This flexibility allows organizations to stay ahead in competitive industries and navigate unexpected disruptions.

The Power of Mentorship

As you continue to grow as a leader, consider the role of mentorship in your journey. Mentorship involves a more experienced individual guiding and supporting someone less experienced. Being both a mentor and a mentee can be exceedingly valuable.

As a mentor, you have the chance to impart your knowledge and experience to others. It's a way to give back to your community and aid the next generation of leaders in succeeding. Mentoring can also provide fresh perspectives and keep you connected to emerging trends and ideas. On the flip side, as a mentee, you can gain wisdom and guidance from someone who has walked the path before you. Seek out mentors who inspire you and can offer insights into areas where you aim to grow as a leader.

Moreover, a part of your legacy can be the development of future leaders. Investing in leadership development programs within your organization guarantees that your influence extends beyond your tenure. It's a method to transmit your knowledge and values to the next generation of leaders.

The Legacy of Leadership

Amidst your leadership journey, it's essential not to overlook work-life balance. The demands of leadership can be all-encompassing, but neglecting your personal life can lead to burnout and diminish your effectiveness as a leader.

The Importance of Continuous Learning

In the ever-evolving landscape of leadership, the pursuit of knowledge is paramount. Effective leaders are lifelong learners who stay informed about industry trends and developments. They understand that to lead successfully, they must remain adaptable and open to new ideas.

Consider investing in your education and professional development. Attend workshops, conferences, and seminars relevant to your field. Read books and articles written by thought leaders in leadership and management. Seek out mentors who can challenge your thinking and provide guidance.

Moreover, don't underestimate the power of informal learning. Conversations with colleagues, exposure to different cultures, and even failures can be valuable sources of learning. Embrace each experience as an opportunity to grow and expand your leadership skills.

The Art of Decision-Making: Navigating the Leadership Landscape

Effective leadership hinges on the art of decision-making. Whether you're leading a small team or steering a large organization, your ability to make sound choices can significantly influence its trajectory. In this exploration of the decision-making process, we will delve deeper into each step outlined above, providing insights, strategies, and real-world examples to help you refine your decision-making prowess.

1.Gather Information: The Foundation of Informed Decisions

The first step in effective decision-making is collecting information. In a world overflowing with data, it's crucial to discern what's relevant.

Access to information has never been easier, but distinguishing between valuable insights and noise remains a challenge.

Leaders should cast a wide net, consulting a range of sources, experts, and team members. Embrace diversity in perspectives and encourage open dialogue. By doing so, you not only gain a comprehensive understanding of the situation but also foster an inclusive decision-making culture.

Consider the instance of Apple Inc. under the leadership of Steve Jobs. When developing the iPhone, Jobs and his team gathered insights from various industries, including the music and telecommunications sectors. This cross-pollination of ideas led to the creation of a groundbreaking product that revolutionized both the smartphone and music industries.

2.Consider Alternatives: Fostering Innovation Through Diverse Solutions

Once you've amassed a trove of information, it's time to explore alternatives. Avoid the trap of fixating on a single solution prematurely. Encourage your team to brainstorm and provide input. Diverse perspectives can lead to more innovative and robust solutions. For instance, consider the story of Netflix. When faced with the declining demand for DVD rentals, the company didn't double down on its existing model. Instead, it explored streaming as an alternative. This bold move paved the way for Netflix's domination of the streaming industry and a shift in how people consume media.

3.Assess Risks and Benefits: Navigating the Path Ahead

Every decision comes with a set of risks and benefits. It's essential to evaluate these thoroughly, considering both short-term and long-term consequences. Effective leaders anticipate potential pitfalls and rewards, balancing the scales to make informed choices.

One prime example is Elon Musk's decision to take Tesla public. This decision carried substantial risks, including market volatility and increased scrutiny. However, Musk believed it was the right path to secure the funding needed to accelerate Tesla's mission of sustainable transportation. Over time, this decision has paid dividends, with Tesla becoming one of the world's most valuable automakers.

4.Trust Your Intuition: The Art of Gut Feelings

While data and analysis are vital, intuition should not be overlooked. Experienced leaders often develop a sense of what's right, honed through years of decision-making. This intuition can serve as a valuable guide, especially in situations where data is limited or inconclusive. Steve Jobs, renowned for his intuitive decision-making, once said, "You have to trust in something – your gut, destiny, life, karma, whatever." Jobs' intuition played a pivotal role in shaping Apple's product lineup and user experience, contributing to its status as an industry leader.

5.Seek Feedback: The Power of Collaborative Wisdom

No leader is an island, and seeking feedback is a cornerstone of effective decision-making. Trusted colleagues, mentors, and team members can provide invaluable insights, challenge your assumptions, and help you uncover blind spots.

Consider the example of the Apollo 13 mission. When faced with a life-threatening crisis in space, NASA's mission control team collaborated closely with engineers and astronauts. Their collective expertise and feedback led to creative solutions that brought the crew safely back to Earth, turning a potential catastrophe into a triumphant return.

6.Make a Decision: The Power of Clarity and Decisiveness

After diligent consideration of information, alternatives, risks, benefits, and intuition, the time comes to make a decision. Indecisiveness can be detrimental to leadership, leading to confusion, stagnation, and missed opportunities.

A classic case of decisive leadership is Abraham Lincoln's Emancipation Proclamation during the American Civil War. Despite immense pressure and controversy, Lincoln made the bold decision to issue the proclamation, which declared that all enslaved people in Confederate-held territory were to be set free. This decision marked a significant turning point in American history, advancing the cause of freedom and equality.

7.Take Responsibility: Embracing the Outcomes

As a leader, taking responsibility for your decisions is non-negotiable. Whether they lead to success or challenges, your decisions shape the course of your organization. It's essential to learn from both positive and negative outcomes, adapting and evolving as a leader.

Consider the example of IBM's CEO, Ginni Rometty. She made the strategic decision to focus the company on cloud computing and artificial intelligence, divesting from less profitable businesses. While this transition faced initial challenges, Rometty's vision and accountability contributed to IBM's resurgence as a leader in the technology industry. Effective leaders recognize that decision-making is not a one-size-fits-all endeavor; it's a dynamic interplay of information, intuition, and collaboration. By embracing these steps and continually refining their decision-making skills, leaders can navigate the complex landscape of leadership with confidence and competence, driving their organizations toward success and innovation.

The Art of Effective Communication

Effective communication is a multifaceted skill that plays a pivotal role in leadership and organizational success. It goes beyond the mere exchange of information; it's the art of connecting, inspiring, and nurturing relationships within your team. To delve deeper into the art of effective communication, we will explore each of the ten key principles outlined above.

1.Clarity:

Clarity is the cornerstone of effective communication. Leaders must convey their messages in a straightforward and easily understandable manner.

Complex jargon and convoluted language can hinder comprehension and breed confusion among team members. By embracing clarity, you ensure your directives are unmistakable, minimizing misunderstandings.

2.Active Listening:

Effective leaders are not just speakers; they are also keen listeners. Active listening involves more than just hearing words; it means empathizing with your team members and acknowledging their viewpoints. By doing so, you nurture an atmosphere of trust and cooperation where everyone feels listened to and appreciated.

3.Feedback:

Feedback serves as a potent instrument for development and progress. Leaders should actively encourage their teams to provide feedback. When delivered with empathy and a growth mindset, constructive criticism can lead to continuous improvement and innovation. It's a pathway to refining both individual and collective performance.

4.Inspiration:

Effective leaders are visionaries. They are passionate about their mission and are adept at sharing their vision and values with contagious enthusiasm. By connecting the daily tasks of your team to a larger purpose, you inspire them to work toward a common goal, igniting motivation and dedication.

5.Adaptability:

Not everyone on your team is the same, and effective communication requires adaptability. Recognize that different team members may respond better to varying communication styles. Being flexible and adjusting your approach to suit individual preferences and needs fosters better understanding and engagement.

6.Transparency:

Transparency is the bedrock of trust and credibility. Leaders should be open and forthright about important decisions, changes, and challenges within the organization. When your team knows that you are honest and forthcoming, it strengthens their trust in your leadership.

7.Non-Verbal Communication:

Communication isn't limited to words alone. Your body language, facial expressions, and tone of voice also convey messages. Being mindful of your non-verbal cues ensures they align with your spoken words. A congruent message fosters clarity and trust.

8.Empowerment:

Effective leaders empower their team members. Encouraging them to convey their notions and take responsibility for their work fosters a culture of ingenuity and engagement. When individuals feel esteemed and authorized, they are more prone to contribute creatively and enthusiastically.

9.Conflict Resolution:

Conflict is inevitable in any group, but it doesn't have to be detrimental. Effective communication skills are crucial in resolving conflicts constructively. By listening actively and using communication as a tool to find common ground, leaders can facilitate resolution and even turn conflicts into opportunities for growth.

10. Continuous Improvement:

Communication, like any skill, can always be refined and enhanced. Seeking feedback on your communication style and actively working on improving it is a hallmark of a great leader. Embrace a growth mindset and view each interaction as an opportunity to become a better communicator. The art of effective communication is an ongoing journey for leaders. It encompasses clarity, active listening, feedback, inspiration, adaptability, transparency, non-verbal communication, empowerment, conflict resolution, and continuous improvement.

Mastering these principles can transform not only your leadership style but also the dynamics within your team, ultimately leading to greater success and fulfillment in your organizational endeavors.

Leading with Humility

Modesty is a trait that differentiates remarkable leaders from merely capable ones. It encompasses recognizing your competencies and deficiencies, confessing when you err, and appreciating the input of others. Humble leaders are approachable and relatable, which fosters a positive team dynamic.

Practice humility by:

1. **Admitting Mistakes:** When you make a mistake, acknowledge it and take responsibility. This demonstrates accountability and builds trust with your team.
2. **Seeking Input:** Value the perspectives and ideas of your team members. Encourage them to share their thoughts and actively listen to their input.
3. **Being Open to Feedback:** Welcome feedback from your team and others. Constructive criticism can help you grow as a leader.

4. **Sharing Credit:** Give recognition where it's merited. Recognize the contributions of your team and commemorate their achievements.

5. **Showing Gratitude:** Convey appreciation for the backing and endeavors of those surrounding you. A simple expression of gratitude can significantly assist in constructing favorable connections.

Leadership and Ethics

Ethical leadership stands as a cornerstone of thriving organizations. As a leader, your resolutions and deeds establish the atmosphere for ethical conduct within your team and corporation. Upholding ethical principles is not solely the ethical thing to do but also indispensable for long-lasting success.

Consider the following ethical principles in your leadership journey:

1. **Integrity:** Maintain honesty and consistency in your actions and decisions. Integrity builds trust with your team and stakeholders.

2. **Fairness:** Treat all team members equitably, without favoritism or discrimination. A fair leader creates a culture of inclusion.

3. **Accountability:** Take responsibility for your actions and decisions. Hold yourself and your team accountable for meeting ethical standards.

4. **Transparency:** Be open and transparent about financial, operational, and ethical matters within your organization. Transparency builds trust and credibility.

5. **Respect:** Show respect for the dignity and rights of all individuals. Respectful leadership fosters a positive and inclusive workplace culture.

6. **Social Responsibility:** Consider the social and environmental impact of your organization's decisions. Ethical leaders aim to make a positive contribution to society.

Leading Through Change

Alteration is an enduring feature in the corporate realm, and leaders must be proficient at steering their teams through it. Whether it's a modification in strategy, technology, or organizational structure, your capability to lead during change can shape your organization's success.

To lead effectively through change:

1. **Communicate Clearly**: Clearly explain the reasons for the change, its expected impact, and the steps involved. Address concerns and questions from your team.

2. **Involve Your Team:** Involve team members in the change process. Encourage their input and ideas for how to navigate the transition.

3. **Provide Support:** Recognize that change can be challenging for individuals. Offer support, resources, and training as needed to help your team adapt.
4. **Be Flexible:** Be open to adjustments and refinements to the change plan as you learn from the process. Flexibility is key in adapting to unforeseen challenges.
5. **Lead by Example:** Demonstrate your commitment to the change by embracing it yourself. Your attitude and actions set the tone for your team.
6. **Monitor Progress:** Continuously assess the progress of the change initiative. Celebrate milestones and address any issues promptly.

The Importance of Self-Care

Leaders frequently concentrate on tending to their teams and organizations, yet prioritizing self-care is equally vital. Your physical and mental well-being directly impact your effectiveness as a leader.

Consider incorporating self-care practices into your routine:

1. **Exercise**: Routine physical activity is crucial for preserving vitality and diminishing stress. Discover a kind of exercise you relish and cultivate it as a routine.

2. **Meditation and Mindfulness:** Meditation and mindfulness can aid you in managing stress, augmenting concentration, and making more astute decisions. Devote a portion of your day to tranquil contemplation.

3. **Healthy Diet:** Proper nutrition fuels your body and mind. Be mindful of your dietary preferences and endeavor for a well-rounded, healthful diet.

4. **Adequate Sleep:** Inadequate sleep can impair decision-making and cognitive function. Prioritize getting enough rest each night.

5. **Disconnect:** Set boundaries for work-related communication outside of working hours. Disconnecting allows you to recharge and maintain a healthy work-life balance.

6. **Hobbies and Interests:** Engage in activities outside of work that bring you joy and relaxation. Hobbies provide an outlet for creativity and stress relief.

The Journey of Personal Growth

Your leadership journey is, in the end, a quest for personal growth. It's about discovering your capabilities, confronting your flaws, and consistently maturing as a leader and as an individual. While thinking about your journey thus far, grasp that leadership is not an endpoint but an enduring pursuit. Embrace each challenge as an opportunity to learn and grow. Seek inspiration from leaders who have left a lasting legacy and use their stories as motivation to continue pushing the boundaries of your own leadership.

In closing, remember that leadership is a dynamic and evolving endeavor. It's about enabling others, fashioning a constructive impact, and leaving behind a legacy of motivation and development. Welcome the difficulties, seize the prospects, and perpetually evolve into the leader you were predestined to be. Your voyage attests to the strength of zeal, resolution, modesty, and continual self-improvement. Persist in motivating those in your vicinity; unitedly, we can mold a brighter tomorrow through exceptional leadership.

Chapter 6: Challenges

Navigating the realm of entrepreneurship as a woman is a journey filled with distinctive challenges and prospects. It's a path that often requires a delicate balance between home life and a thriving career. In this chapter, we'll delve into the intricacies you might encounter along this exceptional journey and equip you with priceless methods to maneuver them. Keep in mind, as women, we are multifaceted individuals who undergo a broad spectrum of emotions throughout our lifetimes, and these emotions can become even more intricate as we mature. Nonetheless, we possess an incredible reservoir of strength and resilience that can see us through any challenge.

Our inherent disposition is often depicted as gentle, but underneath lies an unswerving core of determination and strength. We hold the capability to adapt and persist in the face of adversity. As you embark on your entrepreneurial journey, it's imperative to eradicate the word “no” from your vocabulary. Having faith in yourself and your abilities constitutes the cornerstone of your triumph. To excel in this domain, you must nurture a strong character and maintain unwavering faith in your own judgment because, as a leader, you will confront numerous trials and elevated expectations.

Self-awareness is key. You must intimately understand yourself and your business. Endurance will be your ally because things won't always go according to plan. Welcome imperfections, for the quest for flawlessness is an endless expedition. Behind the scenes, you may face hindrances and setbacks, but remember your audience only perceives what you want to present to them.

When faced with challenges, avoid dwelling on the problem. Redirect your energy toward finding solutions. Take the time to introspect and reflect, but never entertain the notion of giving up. Each hurdle should be embraced as an opportunity to grow and evolve, allowing your entrepreneurial spirit to soar to new heights.

This counsel is not restricted to women alone; it is a universal principle anyone can adopt. Surround yourself with individuals who endorse your aspirations and appreciate your endeavors. Life is too short to accompany someone who doesn't align with your goals, regardless of gender.

Building self-confidence is a process fraught with trials, including instances of self-doubt and external detractors. Nevertheless, it is imperative to remain steadfast in your dedication to your objectives, even if that entails advancing independently at times. Continually remind yourself of your internal strength and persistence, knowing you possess the capacity to overcome any challenges that lie ahead.

As we alter our perspective on challenges, we discern they need not burden us; instead, they can function as stepping stones toward discovering solutions. Trusting in ourselves is paramount, as it empowers us to handle whatever life throws our way. When we grasp this concept and recognize our self-worth, we become unstoppable.

Reaching the point of unwavering self-acceptance denotes a momentous transformation. At this juncture, we begin to perceive the world and its inhabitants as they genuinely are. By standing firm and refusing to compromise our values, we unlock boundless opportunities.

The root of the problem doesn't stem from undervaluing ourselves but from placing excessive expectations on others. When we fully embrace our uniqueness and accept ourselves unconditionally, we become emboldened and manifest our remarkable selves.

Acknowledging the significance of time and fostering self-confidence paves the way for both success and happiness. We should continually progress, explore, and leave a positive mark, recognizing our potential to excel in all life's facets.

Achieving success is a significant accomplishment that requires determination, resilience, and unwavering commitment. It involves hard work and overcoming challenges, but refusing to surrender can make all the difference. With dedication, guidance, and self-assurance, success becomes attainable. Remaining steadfast in our objectives is vital because restarting can feel arduous and demoralizing.

Bear in mind that success isn't always effortless. Even in moments of uncertainty, it's essential to remain resolute and avoid giving up. Trusting in oneself and bolstering self-esteem are pivotal to achieving greatness. Staying true to oneself and resisting external influences is imperative. In the professional realm, you may encounter critics or individuals attempting to undermine your progress. However, upholding your authenticity and not allowing others to shape your identity is essential. How do you confront these challenges and stay motivated? Let's delve deeper into aspects of this extraordinary journey and elaborate on techniques to navigate them.

1. Balancing Home and Career:

Striking a balance between home and your career can be demanding, yet vital for overall well-being and success. To attain this balance, adhere to these guidelines:

a) Establish Clear Boundaries:

- Define your work hours and personal time.
- Communicate these boundaries to colleagues and superiors.

b) Craft a Structured Schedule:

- Organize your day to encompass work, leisure, family time, and self-care.
- Allocate specific time slots for each facet of your life.

c) Prioritize Tasks:

- Identify top-priority tasks and focus on them.
- Consider delegating less critical tasks to others.

d) Seek Support:

- Don't hesitate to seek assistance from family, partners, or childcare services.

Balancing your career and personal life is a continuous journey. By following these strategies and maintaining flexibility, you can attain improved well-being and success in both domains.

2. Embracing Emotions:

Emotions constitute a pivotal element of personal growth and well-being, particularly for women.

Like everyone else, women experience a wide array of emotions stemming from various sources, including personal experiences, societal pressures, and hormonal fluctuations. It's vital to recognize that emotions aren't indicative of weakness; they are an innate aspect of human nature.

The initial step toward emotional well-being entails acknowledging these emotions.

Many women face societal pressures to conceal their feelings or conform to traditional notions of femininity, which wrongly suggest that emotional expression signifies vulnerability. However, embracing emotions involves acknowledging their validity and importance.

Emotions provide insight into our needs, desires, and boundaries, aiding women in better understanding themselves. Moreover, cultivating emotional intelligence is valuable for women across various life domains. Emotional intelligence entails recognizing, comprehending, managing, and effectively utilizing emotions. It empowers women to make informed decisions in their personal and professional lives. In the workplace, emotional intelligence facilitates women in navigating social dynamics, resolving conflicts, and communicating effectively with colleagues and superiors.

In relationships, emotional intelligence is indispensable for establishing strong and meaningful connections. It allows women to empathize with others, engage in active listening, and respond empathetically to the emotions of their partners, friends, and family members. This fosters trust and intimacy and strengthens the bonds between individuals. Furthermore, embracing emotions empowers women to be advocates for themselves and others. It equips them with the ability to stand against injustices, articulate their needs, and champion gender equality. Emotions can serve as a driving force for positive change, motivating women to take action and make a difference in their communities and the world. Embracing emotions is a testament to strength and resilience, not weakness. It's a potent tool that assists women in understanding themselves, making informed choices, building meaningful relationships, and advocating for themselves and others. By recognizing the value of their emotions and nurturing emotional intelligence, women can tap into their inner strength and navigate life's challenges with authenticity and grace.

3. The Power of Self-Belief:

Believing in oneself is paramount in entrepreneurship. The business landscape is rife with challenges and uncertainties, and self-confidence is the compass that keeps you on course. Success often resides beyond your comfort zone, necessitating the willingness to take risks and embrace the unknown, which can lead to growth and opportunities.

Fostering self-belief is a gradual process. It entails recognizing your strengths and weaknesses, learning from missteps, and maintaining faith in your capacity to adapt. Self-compassion is equally vital, especially when things deviate from the plan.

You are not alone in your entrepreneurial voyage. Surrounding yourself with mentors and peers can yield remarkable benefits. Mentors offer invaluable advice based on their experiences, aiding you in navigating hurdles. Peers offer companionship and a sense of community, which can be motivating and reassuring.

Self-belief constitutes the cornerstone of entrepreneurship, emboldening you to step outside your comfort zone, exhibit resilience, and confront the unpredictable nature of business. When coupled with self-compassion and a supportive network, it forms a robust foundation for pursuing entrepreneurial aspirations and attaining success.

4. Adapting to Challenges:

Entrepreneurship is a journey fraught with ups and downs, and confronting challenges is an integral part of it. These challenges might encompass financial aspects, evolving markets, competition, or unforeseen events such as a pandemic. Flourishing in this ever-changing landscape hinges on adaptability.

It entails remaining flexible and open to change. It revolves around modifying your business strategy when necessary, whether by altering your offerings, exploring new markets, or adjusting your business model to align with the prevailing circumstances. Savvy entrepreneurs understand that adhering rigidly to a plan during trying times can culminate in failure. Instead, they perceive change as an opportunity for growth and innovation.

Setbacks are common in entrepreneurship but should not be viewed as failures. Consider them opportunities for learning. Each challenge encountered imparts valuable insights, enables business refinement, and cultivates new skills. Overcoming these obstacles aids in refining strategies, identifying weaknesses, and discovering strengths.

Resilience stands as a pivotal trait for entrepreneurs. It encompasses bouncing back from setbacks and persisting onward. Even when adversity looms, maintaining a positive attitude and unwavering determination can yield significant differences. Resilience empowers you to endure even the most trying of times.

5. Embracing Imperfection:

Embracing imperfection bears significance, not only for entrepreneurs but for individuals across the board. The pursuit of perfection is often frustrating and unattainable. Instead, emphasizes progress and continuous improvement, which is particularly advantageous for entrepreneurs.

Entrepreneurs grapple with distinct challenges in an ever-changing world and will undoubtedly encounter setbacks. Nevertheless, these setbacks serve as opportunities for learning and improvement rather than constituting failures. This realization can mitigate the fear of failure.

Understanding that even accomplished individuals and organizations commit errors can invigorate entrepreneurs with greater determination and resilience.

In entrepreneurship, it is imperative to acknowledge imperfections as integral to the journey. This mindset fosters creativity and innovation since individuals are more willing to experiment, take risks, and explore novel concepts without the apprehension of making mistakes.

Furthermore, embracing imperfections enhances adaptability. Enterprises must evolve with the times, and entrepreneurs who embrace imperfections are flexible when faced with change. They can adjust their strategies based on feedback and data, a vital skill in a competitive market.

6. Authenticity and Transparency:

Authenticity and transparency serve as the cornerstones for building trust and credibility in today's interconnected world. Authenticity revolves around remaining true to oneself, aligning actions with values and beliefs, and showcasing one's real identity. Transparency, on the other hand, entails being open and honest, refraining from concealing information or intentions. When transparent, you share pertinent details and context, aiding others in comprehending your actions and decisions.

In personal branding or professional communication, authenticity and transparency wield significant influence. Authenticity involves embracing your uniqueness and refraining from pretense or adopting masks to fit in. This authenticity can attract like-minded individuals who share your values and beliefs, laying the groundwork for meaningful relationships grounded in trust.

Additionally, being transparent about your journey is of paramount importance. Sharing both successes and setbacks serves as a source of inspiration while also demonstrating your commitment to growth and learning. Success stories inspire, but the willingness to acknowledge when things deviate from the plan makes you relatable. It conveys that you are not infallible but resolute in your pursuit of improvement.

By embracing authenticity and transparency, you construct a solid foundation for trust and credibility. People value those who are genuine and forthright, making them more inclined to offer support. In an age characterized by skepticism, these qualities set you apart and facilitate the formation of enduring connections, as well as the realization of your objectives. Therefore, prioritize authenticity and transparency in your interactions and communications to nurture the flourishing of trust and credibility.

7. Building a Supportive Network:

Establishing a supportive network proves indispensable for personal and professional triumph. The individuals in your circle wield considerable influence over your journey toward your goals. Consequently, connecting with individuals who share your beliefs and aspirations is pivotal. These individuals form the bedrock of your support system, offering encouragement and motivation.

One key facet of constructing such a network is locating mentors and peers. Mentors proffer invaluable insights and guidance rooted in their experiences, assisting you in sidestepping common pitfalls and surmounting challenges. Interacting with peers facilitates the exchange of ideas and mutual support as they traverse comparable paths.

Peers, too, hold substantial significance. They confront similar challenges and opportunities, and bonding with them offers a platform for learning from their experiences, in addition to mutual support. The camaraderie among peers can be motivating and reassuring.

However, it is also imperative to discern and disengage from individuals who impede your progress. Periodically, certain individuals may not align with your vision or may introduce negativity into your life. It is imperative to make the challenging decision to distance yourself from such individuals, as their influence can prove detrimental to your growth and success.

8. Staying Focused on Your Goals:

In the realm of entrepreneurship, staying focused on your goals stands as a linchpin for success. The journey unfolds unpredictably, replete with distractions and setbacks. Nevertheless, preserving a clear vision remains paramount for triumph.

Setbacks constitute normal occurrences and offer opportunities for growth. When you deviate from your path, consider it a learning opportunity. Analyze the root causes of the deviation to refine your approach.

Fear, at times, may create a challenging obstacle. Thus, prioritize your mental and emotional well-being. Persevere in concentrating on your goals and contemplate mentorship as a two-way street; being a mentor holds inestimable value and has the potential to inspire many.

Entrepreneurship remains an exciting endeavor, and as a woman, you infuse your distinctive qualities into the equation. We shall explore the challenges and opportunities confronting women in entrepreneurship and expound upon techniques for navigating this gratifying path.

The Strength Within:

During a period when women's potential is frequently underestimated, recognizing the inherent strength within us takes on paramount importance. The notion that women are fragile constitutes a superficial stereotype that fails to acknowledge our tenacity and resilience. Our strength is not confined to the physical realm; it encompasses determination, courage, and unwavering persistence.

Embarking on an entrepreneurial journey is no easy feat; it demands courage and conviction. Female entrepreneurs may encounter skepticism, bias, and discrimination, but these challenges must not deter them. Instead, let these hurdles serve as fuel for your determination. Embrace your inner strength to steer you through arduous times.

To succeed in entrepreneurship, cultivating a robust character is imperative. This involves building resilience, learning from failures, and pushing the boundaries of your capabilities. It necessitates taking risks, making tough decisions, and standing by them. True leadership emerges from such experiences.

In the entrepreneurial sphere, leadership comes laden with lofty expectations and challenges. Nonetheless, it is not about conforming to someone else's notion of leadership; it revolves around embracing your unique qualities and strengths. Your entrepreneurial journey mirrors your inner strength and capacity to adapt, innovate, and inspire.

Self-Awareness and Endurance:

Self-awareness and endurance serve as critical assets for entrepreneurial success.

Self-awareness entails understanding your strengths, weaknesses, values, and motivations. This equips you to make informed decisions aligned with your objectives and to identify your unique strengths, enabling the construction of an authentic business. Self-awareness also aids in forming a well-rounded team.

Endurance signifies the ability to persevere in the face of adversity. Entrepreneurship presents both highs and lows, but enduring challenges is pivotal. Embrace imperfections and concentrate on continuous improvement.

Furthermore, projecting a favorable image to your audience is vital. While you confront challenges, your audience observes your polished business persona. Maintain professionalism, transparency, and consistency. Exhibit resilience and problem-solving skills when confronted with difficulties.

Overcoming Setbacks:

Remaining focused on your goals remains paramount to overcoming setbacks. Temporarily straying from your path or encountering unforeseen obstacles is plausible, but success favors those who rediscover their trajectory and maintain an unwavering commitment to their vision, irrespective of the hurdles.

Embracing Challenges:

To effectively tackle challenges, introspect and scrutinize your strengths and weaknesses. Probe the root causes of issues to gain a deeper understanding. In your pursuit of entrepreneurship, consider the following strategies to confront and overcome challenges effectively:

1. **Problem-Solving Mindset:** Cultivate a problem-solving mindset. View challenges as opportunities to innovate and improve. Break down complex issues into manageable components and systematically work through them. Collaborate with your team to brainstorm creative solutions.
2. **Continuous Learning:** Embrace a mindset of continuous learning. Seek out knowledge and expertise in areas where you encounter challenges. Attend workshops, seminars, or online courses to acquire new skills. Engage with mentors who can provide valuable insights.
3. **Resilience:** Resilience is your ally when facing adversity. Understand that setbacks are part of the entrepreneurial journey. When faced with failure or obstacles, don't dwell on them excessively. Instead,

extract lessons from these experiences and use them to refine your approach.

4. **Effective Communication:** Communication is vital in navigating challenges. Clearly articulate the issues you're facing to your team, mentors, or support network. Effective communication fosters collaboration and can lead to innovative solutions.

5. **Adaptability:** The business landscape is dynamic. Be prepared to adapt your strategies and business model as needed. Agility is a valuable trait that enables you to respond effectively to changing circumstances.

6. **Networking:** Leverage your network for support and guidance. Engage with fellow entrepreneurs, industry experts, and mentors. They can offer valuable advice, share their experiences, and provide a fresh perspective on your challenges.

7. **Time Management:** Efficient time management is crucial when tackling challenges. Prioritize tasks, set realistic deadlines, and allocate your resources wisely. Avoid spreading yourself too thin and focus on the most pressing issues first.

8. **Self-Care:** Don't underestimate the importance of self-care. Entrepreneurship can be demanding, both mentally and physically. Take time to recharge, practice stress management techniques, and maintain a healthy work-life balance.

9. **Data-Driven Decision-Making:** Use data to inform your decisions. Analyze market trends, customer feedback, and financial metrics to gain insights into your challenges. Data-driven decision-making can lead to more informed and effective solutions.

10. **Persistence:** Persistence is often the key to overcoming the toughest challenges. Stay committed to your goals and keep moving forward, even when faced with setbacks. Remember that many successful entrepreneurs have faced numerous obstacles before achieving their goals.

11. **Seeking Guidance:** Don't hesitate to seek guidance from experienced mentors or advisors. They can provide valuable insights and help you navigate complex challenges more effectively.

12. **Collaboration:** Consider collaboration as a strategy to overcome challenges. Partnering with other businesses or individuals who complement your strengths can lead to innovative solutions.

13. **Mindset Shift:** Shift your mindset from viewing challenges as roadblocks to seeing them as opportunities for growth. Embrace a growth mindset that welcomes learning and development through adversity.

14. **Celebrate Small Wins:** Recognize and celebrate small victories along the way. Acknowledging your

progress, no matter how incremental, can boost morale and motivation.

15. **Stay Informed**: Stay informed about industry trends, changes in regulations, and emerging technologies. Being proactive in anticipating challenges can give you a competitive edge.

Remember that every challenge you encounter is a chance to learn, adapt, and grow. As a woman in entrepreneurship, you bring unique perspectives and strengths to the table. Embrace these qualities, stay resilient, and continue your journey with confidence and determination. Success often lies on the other side of the challenges you face.

Let's take a look at my expeditions.

In my journey through life, I have come to a profound realization: time is an invaluable asset, and as I grow older, its significance becomes clearer. I have realized that I must not let anyone or anything waste my time, as it has immense value. My appreciation for my time has allowed me to detect the true motives of those around me, including my spouse.

In my twenties, I had not yet developed the insight I now have in my fifth decade. On reflection, I realize I could have done more to improve my personal life as well as my business decisions. I squandered precious energy and period on the incorrect activities, overlooking what had real significance to me. Sadly, my lack of self-belief confused me, and I permitted others to shape my actions and choices.

Realizing the significance of recognizing oneself and being around those who have the same targets and aspirations is something I only came to find out late in life. Not everyone is expected to take the same route or occupy a similar position in life. Acknowledging this fact empowers us to concentrate on our voyage. It wasn't until I was in my thirties that I understood this seminal lesson properly.

I must emphasize that success does not come without struggles. I have come to comprehend that my course was not intended for everybody. It takes guts and the disposition to lean on those around me for help when I truly need it. I frequently became uncertain and experienced difficulty, yet those around me gave me the strength and support to keep going.

My mother, a Leo like myself, is a born leader who never gives up. She was a single parent to four kids after breaking away from my dad. Her courage and toughness impressed me profoundly, and I felt deeply connected to her. Despite the setbacks she was met with, she did wonderful work parenting us.

My mother often expressed how much we resembled each other and would remind me of the great potential she saw in me. At 19 years old, she saw that I had the potential to spur others on by starting my own company and buying my first home when I was 21. Even though I was unaware of my influence on those around me, she thought it was notable.

She encouraged me not to settle but to continue striving for success and to use my blessings to help others. Reflecting on those challenging times, I appreciated the wisdom my mother imparted. Material possessions lost their significance when I was at my lowest, and it's up to me to use them and bring out my true worth. My mother was the one who helped me realize that the real riches reside in what we can do, our individual talents and skills. She instilled in me that I hold the key to a successful life in my mind and hands, and it is up to me to utilize them and demonstrate my value. With my skills and abilities, I can venture anywhere and achieve financial prosperity. These words of wisdom from my mother resonated deeply within me, opening my eyes to my true potential.

It's fascinating how people idolize money but struggle to understand the art of creating it. My mother, however, saw something special in me – the ability to generate income seemingly out of thin air. At that moment, I was not completely aware of this present. However, her advice aided me in comprehending reality.

I had no idea when I was 15 that all I had was my talents and abilities. I was aware, though, of how important what I had was, and I was determined to use it to its fullest capacity.

My mother's belief in me boosted my confidence and triggered a revelation. She illuminated my path, making me aware of my untapped potential. From then on, I was determined to rise from my lowest point and continue forging ahead, knowing that the only way was up.

Undoubtedly, there have been challenges along the way, small hurdles, and setbacks. Nevertheless, each experience taught me a valuable lesson – I can endure anything that comes my way.

I discovered a vital lesson during a difficult time in a failed relationship. I realized that I must love myself above all else. I must take action to protect myself from being taken advantage of and accept anything less than I am worth.

I practiced glancing into the mirror daily and saying "I love you" to bolster my self-esteem and become confident in my worth. This act of self-love allowed me to distance myself from toxic interactions and step toward a positive future. I am now proud of my capabilities and inspired to take advantage of whatever opportunities are presented to me. Having received my mother's encouragement and acknowledging myself as a capable person, I no longer succumb to apprehension or hesitation. I remain confident about my voyage ahead, secure in my faith in myself, and committed to succeeding in anything I pursue.

In my mind and within my grasp lies the key to success. My skills and abilities empower me to venture into uncharted territories and achieve financial prosperity. These invaluable words of wisdom from my mother have profoundly resonated within me, igniting a realization of my true potential. It's intriguing to witness how people idolize money while struggling to grasp the art of its creation. However, my mother saw something exceptional in me – the ability to generate income seemingly out of thin air. I didn't fully comprehend this gift at that moment, but her guidance gradually unveiled the truth. My mother used to tell me to be nice to those who didn't like me, to greet them with a smile and friendly hello. This approach might seem unconventional, but it takes away their joy when they realize their negativity doesn't affect you. In the past, I have encountered people who pretended to be encouraging but secretly worked against me. Rather than completely eliminating them, I kept going and focused on what I wanted to achieve.

In my world, negativity has no place. I believe that problems are only problems if we allow them to be. When my team comes to me with an issue, I encourage them to present a solution. Dwelling on problems without seeking resolutions only depletes our energy and accomplishes nothing. In my professional journey, I embrace a 100% positive outlook. As team players, we always collaborate effectively. However, living together is not a mandatory requirement. If there's a person that you do not vibe with, that's fine. Note that it is a symbol of strength to recognize and honor differences.

Rather than worrying, let's look for ways to make things better. A beam of positivity from a simple smile can have a profound effect, brightening the hours and boosting energy. I am confident that everything comes with a solution. I have encountered numerous challenges but have always found a way out. When one door closes, I seek another and create a new path to success.

Chapter 7: Overcoming Obstacles and Building a Strong Team

After successfully starting your business, it's crucial to face and conquer the obstacles that come your way. Although these challenges might seem difficult, remember that you have the strength and ability to overcome them. With each obstacle conquered, you'll find yourself breathing a little easier. Things would flow more smoothly now, particularly in those initial years when you were solely responsible for managing your enterprise.

As your business expands, the need for additional staff becomes paramount. This step holds significant importance. Initially, you might start with W-9 or 1099 workers, eventually transitioning to W-2 employees, especially as your business undergoes incorporation. This transition signifies a shift in your business operations.

Building Your Team

While building your team, exercise caution and be selective. Hiring dedicated and loyal staff members is the linchpin to your business's success. However, assembling this team is no simple task. Although websites advertising job positions might be helpful, it's not always as straightforward as it seems. When utilizing such platforms, ensure that you precisely describe the job title and responsibilities.

Engaging a headhunter or a staffing agency could be beneficial in certain instances. These avenues can assist you in locating candidates who perfectly align with the job description you're seeking to fill. This approach might simplify the process of finding the right fit for your team.

Remember, your journey as a business owner is an ongoing evolution. Embrace the bumps and bruises as opportunities for growth, and maintain your focus on assembling a team that shares your dedication and loyalty. By doing this, you're boosting your business and creating an atmosphere of drive and accomplishment.

Hiring Friends and Family

When establishing a thriving enterprise, many suggest it is prudent to consider employing close acquaintances or relatives. However, my stance is not a steadfast endorsement of this approach. Those you bring on board must share the same business goals and are prepared to differentiate between familial dynamics and professional expectations.

In essence, your family members or friends must recognize the distinction between their role as employees within your business and their role in personal matters. They should comprehend that while you might share a familial bond, you hold the position of authority in the workplace, and they are accountable for contributing to the business's success. This understanding extends to pay, salary, and wages; they must grasp these concepts beyond the confines of family relationships. Indeed, they must be able to differentiate between these aspects. Yet, I've consistently found the task of intertwining family ties with business operations challenging. It's important to note that my experience might not universally apply, as some individuals may have found harmonious ways to blend family and business.

Regardless of whether you choose to hire family members, the key lies in cultivating an environment that is firm and compassionate. Communicate your business objectives, values, and expectations. Your dedication to the business's prosperity should be evident, and potential employees should perceive the opportunity for personal and professional growth through their involvement with your venture.

Maintaining a sense of structure, organization, and clear boundaries is paramount. Uphold your standards consistently and remain resolute in pursuing your goals. Following these guidelines establishes the foundation for a prosperous business path. Nevertheless, it's important to recognize that locating the proper match for your team may involve a certain amount of experimentation.

Team Building and Recognition

When building a great team, you might have to work with various people, including employees and freelancers, until you find the right fit for your goals and needs. Staff turnover is a reality in many businesses, and this process can be trying. However, it is crucially important to concentrate on the broader perspective and the ultimate aim of establishing a united and effective group. The decision of whether to hire family members or friends for your business is a nuanced one. While some advocate for this approach, I believe potential hires must share their business aspirations and comprehend the professional dynamics involved. Mixing family matters with business operations can be complicated, and it's essential to establish a clean and respectful environment.

Irrespective of your hiring choices, fostering a balance between firmness, kindness, and transparent communication is pivotal. Embrace a structured approach, remain steadfast in your goals, and anticipate that finding the right team members may involve some turnover. Ultimately, your commitment to these principles will greatly impact the success of your business.

The Power of a Positive Mindset

In the constantly evolving business world, it's important to maintain a positive mindset by remembering that good things are coming soon. Knowing that there is hope can be a source of comfort during difficult times. Additionally, it's comforting to know that others out there have the same strong dedication to their work and are prepared to go on this journey with you.

Your dreams and business goals are worth pursuing with unwavering determination. Persistence is key, and just when you start to doubt, the universe can surprise you. It's at the moments when you least anticipate it that the perfect individual will walk through that door, bringing with them the skillset and attitude that aligns perfectly with your needs.

People of this caliber are rare gems you hold dear to your heart. They are the rocks of help, standing tall no matter the difficulties that arise. They don't just work for you; they become vital to your goal. These individuals have the potential to nurture your enterprise as if it were their very own.

Nurturing Exceptional Employees

It's essential to nurture these exceptional employees. Such loyalty and dedication don't materialize often. Offer them opportunities to showcase their talents and prove their mettle. You're sowing the seeds of mutual respect and lasting partnership by granting them the chance to thrive. As they pour their heart and soul into their work, reciprocate by acknowledging their efforts.

Recognition takes various forms, all originating from a place of genuine appreciation. Let your gratitude reflect in the tokens of recognition you bestow upon them.

The heartfelt meaning of rewards, whether a recognition for exceptional commitment or a simple gesture of kindness, cannot be underestimated. Remember that the reward's value lies not in its size or cost but in its genuine sentiment. When you give, let it come from a place of sincerity. Your employees can sense authenticity; your acknowledgment will carry more weight when you truly value their contributions. These actions foster a sense of belonging and empowerment within your team. They'll know their hard work isn't just noticed; it's celebrated.

The Impact of Appreciation

The impact of your appreciation isn't limited to the immediate moment. Its ripples extend far and wide, touching the core of your workforce. By acknowledging their toil and commitment, you're nurturing an environment of mutual support and growth. In recognizing their worth, you're laying the foundation for a team that thrives collectively.

Never underestimate the power of a united team. Feeling seen and valued, your employees will rise to the occasion with even greater zeal. The realization that their efforts drive the business's success fuels their determination. Acknowledging their contribution instills a sense of purpose that's hard to replicate elsewhere.

Your Unwavering Commitment

As the business evolves and transforms, these exceptional individuals will stand steadfastly by your side. Their loyalty, fortified by your acknowledgment and care, isn't fleeting. They'll weather storms and share in the triumphs, consistently committed to the growth and prosperity of your enterprise. In the grand tapestry of your journey, these team members are the threads that hold it all together. Cherish them, for they are the embodiment of your vision and aspirations. Nurture their growth, celebrate their successes, and stand by their side as they stand by yours. Remember, the path to success is a collaborative one. While it's your dream that propels the journey, it's their dedication that fuels its momentum.

With appreciation as the cornerstone of your interactions, these individuals will become the backbone of your business. And over time, you'll discover that their unwavering support and dedication last not just for a few years but throughout every step of your adventure.

The Unwavering Focus and Determination

In the pursuit of your goals, my advice is to maintain unwavering focus and unrelenting motivation. It's important to acknowledge that challenges like towering mountains on your path will arise. This journey is far from easy, demanding your determination and perseverance.

However, when your heart is set on this endeavor, it intertwines with your existence. It becomes an integral part of your daily life, an embodiment that echoes every moment – every minute, every second, every hour. Embracing this aspiration means internalizing it, allowing it to define you. With this conviction, you find the strength to persist, refusing to be swayed by anyone or anything obstructing your way. Your victory in this venture is not just a distant goal but a constant presence. It's a reality that resonates within you and an identity forged through resilience and unwavering commitment. This profound realization propels you forward, rendering giving up inconceivable. You are driven by an unyielding resolve, fortified by the knowledge that your journey cannot be halted.

The Solo Moments of Strength

In this quest, there may not always be a privilege of having a helpful team or a reliable group with you. There will be instances when it's only you facing difficult circumstances. However, this should not discourage you; instead, it's a chance to access your source of drive. In these moments, you become your supporter, reminding yourself of your goal and the enthusiasm propelling your dreams forward.

Remember that specific things are better to be kept to yourself. Some challenges are supposed to be faced privately, deep within your thoughts and emotions. This highlights your inner power, reminding you of your ability to empower yourself. By overcoming these personal obstacles, you acquire the skill of self-encouragement and develop a strength that persists even during tough times.

Although it is great to have people who support and help you, there may be times when you have to depend on your own determination. This is completely fine. Understand that not everyone will be there for you, which can be difficult but not impossible to overcome. Despite everything, you stay loyal to your beliefs and chosen path. Your integrity remains unblemished as you navigate through various influences and opinions.

Your Unique Story

Amidst the unpredictable journey, remember that this is your story to tell. Your life story is made up of the moments that shaped you - the ups, the downs, and everything in between. It's a powerful reminder of how strong you are and of your incredible ability to conquer any obstacle that comes your way.

No matter what hurdles arise, you retain an unshakeable resolve. You stay focused on your goals with unwavering determination, and your belief in yourself helps you keep moving forward. Your dedication and relentless spirit define this adventure.

Embrace the truth that success is not a distant dream but an inevitable reality. It's not an elusive concept; it's a destination you're relentlessly journeying toward. With each step forward, you sculpt your destiny, materializing your aspirations into tangible achievements.

The Strength in Adversity

Your strength prevails in the face of challenges, uncertainties, and setbacks. You remain steadfast in your pursuit, unstayed by the turbulence around you. Your conviction and resilience shine brightly, lighting the path to your ultimate success. Remember, you are the architect of your journey, and your unwavering determination will guide you through every obstacle toward the triumph that awaits. As you continue to navigate the ever-changing landscape of entrepreneurship, remember that obstacles are not roadblocks but stepping stones to your success. They test your mettle, fortify your resolve, and shape you into a formidable business owner. Embrace the journey, build your dream team with care, and know that your unwavering determination will carry you through the challenges and into a future filled with achievement and fulfillment.

In your entrepreneurial story, each chapter is a testament to your dedication, resilience, and unwavering commitment. So, write your unique story, and let your journey inspire others to embark on their own path of determination and success.

The Power of Perseverance

Perseverance is the thread that weaves through the fabric of your entrepreneurial journey. It's the tenacity to keep moving forward, even when faced with seemingly insurmountable obstacles. This quality sets successful business owners apart from the rest.

In the realm of entrepreneurship, there are no certainties. Obstacles are unavoidable, and setbacks will examine your determination. Nevertheless, during these trying moments, your resolve shines most brilliantly. When you persevere, you demonstrate to yourself and others that you are resolute in your dedication to your objectives.

Every setback presents a chance to learn and evolve. It's an opportunity to refine your strategies, adjust to shifting circumstances, and emerge more robust than previously.

Keep in mind that the most accomplished entrepreneurs aren't those who evade failure but those who derive lessons from it and employ it as a stepping stone to triumph.

Adaptation and Resilience

Adaptability is a vital characteristic of any entrepreneur. The business landscape is dynamic, and the capacity to adjust to evolving conditions is crucial. Your journey might necessitate pivoting, reevaluating your business model, or exploring novel prospects.

Resilience is closely intertwined with adaptation. It's the ability to rebound from setbacks and persevere steadfastly toward your goals. Resilience empowers you to weather storms, surmount adversity, and emerge stronger on the other side.

Remember that even the most thriving businesses have faced adversity. What distinguishes them is their resilience and their readiness to evolve in response to changing circumstances. Embrace change as an avenue for growth and view challenges as milestones on your course to success.

Continuous Learning

The entrepreneurial journey is a continuous learning process. As your business evolves, so should your knowledge and skills. Stay curious, seek out new information, and be open to acquiring new skills. Learning from both success and failure is imperative. When things go well, take the time to discern what led to that success and replicate it. When confronted with failure, analyze the root causes and harness that knowledge to make more judicious decisions in the future.

Moreover, contemplate engaging mentors or advisors who can offer guidance and share their experiences. Learning from those who have already traveled your path can be invaluable.

Building a Support System

While unwavering determination is crucial, you don't have to navigate the entrepreneurial journey in solitude. Constructing a support network can supply you with the encouragement, counsel, and perspective you require for success.

Your support network can encompass mentors, fellow entrepreneurs, friends, and family. These individuals can provide guidance, lend a sympathetic ear during trying times, and commemorate your achievements with you. Don't hesitate to reach out to them when you need support or a fresh outlook.

Networking within your industry or entrepreneurial community can also be beneficial. Connecting with others who share your passion and drive can lead to valuable collaborations and partnerships.

The Legacy of Your Entrepreneurial Journey

Every step you take in your entrepreneurial journey leaves a lasting impression, not solely on your business but also on the world around you. Your actions, determination, and unwavering commitment contribute to a legacy that extends beyond your business's confines.

Your journey serves as an inspiration to those aspiring to follow in your footsteps. As you surmount obstacles, navigate challenges, and achieve success, you establish a model for others to emulate. You become a symbol of hope and proof that dreams can materialize through sheer determination and diligent effort.

Creating Opportunities for Others

One of the most rewarding facets of entrepreneurship is the ability to create opportunities for others. As your business flourishes, you possess the capacity to employ individuals, bestow meaningful work upon them, and bolster their professional and personal development.

The individuals you bring into your team become part of your journey. Their dedication and contributions fuel the success of your business. By offering them opportunities and nurturing their talents, you benefit your own enterprise and enrich the lives and careers of those you employ.

Fulfillment and Satisfaction

Entrepreneurship doesn't solely pertain to individual success; it also encompasses contributing to society's greater good. Through your business, you hold the potential to craft products or services that enhance people's lives, address societal dilemmas, and enhance the world's condition.

Your impact extends to your community, industry, and even the global arena. As you contemplate your journey, bear in mind that the pursuit of excellence is an unceasing endeavor. It's evidence of your resilience and unwavering commitment to your vision.

Contributing to Society

Entrepreneurship isn't just about individual success; it's also about contributing to the greater good of society. Through your business, you have the potential to create products or services that improve people's lives, address societal challenges, and make the world a better place.

Your impact extends to your community, industry, and even the global landscape. Your business can drive innovation, create jobs, and inspire positive change. By staying committed to your entrepreneurial journey, you play a role in shaping a brighter future.

The Continued Quest for Excellence

As you reflect on your journey, remember that the pursuit of excellence is an ongoing endeavor. Your unwavering determination has brought you this far and will continue guiding you toward fresh horizons and soaring accomplishments. Embrace each day as an occasion to learn, evolve, and refine your competencies. Stay attuned to fluctuating market dynamics, emerging trends, and evolving customer needs. Adapt, innovate, and continue striving for excellence in all that you do.

Your Legacy of Determination

Your entrepreneurial journey is a testament to your determination, resilience, and unwavering commitment. It's a chronicle of triumph amid adversity, growth amidst challenges, and unceasing pursuit of your dreams.

As you continue writing the chapters of your entrepreneurial narrative, recognize that your legacy extends far beyond the confines of your business. You motivate others, generate opportunities, contribute to society, and discover profound satisfaction in the process. Think about how you can challenge the status quo, introduce innovative solutions, and make a meaningful difference. Your unwavering determination can be the driving force behind transformative change.

With each obstacle you overcome, with each goal you achieve, you leave an enduring legacy of determination—one that serves as a beacon of hope and a testament to the incredible power of unwavering commitment. So, keep moving forward, keep dreaming big, and keep making your mark on the world through your unwavering determination.

Leaving a Lasting Impact on Your Industry

Your journey as an entrepreneur bears the potential to leave a lasting impact, not solely on your business but also on your entire industry. Through your innovative ideas, commitment to excellence, and willingness to take calculated risks, you can establish new standards and motivate others to follow suit.

Consider the trailblazers and visionaries who have reshaped their industries - Steve Jobs in technology, Elon Musk in electric vehicles and space exploration, or Oprah Winfrey in media and entertainment. These individuals didn't just establish prosperous businesses; they transformed entire sectors and reshaped the way we live and work.

Mentoring and Empowering the Next Generation

One of the most potent means to broaden the reach of your entrepreneurial journey is by mentoring and empowering the next generation of aspiring business proprietors. Your experiences, victories, and setbacks contain valuable lessons that can guide and inspire others.

Consider initiating mentorship programs, disseminating your insights through speaking engagements, or chronicling your entrepreneurial voyage in books or articles. In doing so, you can equip others with the knowledge and mindset needed to embark on their entrepreneurial endeavors. Your counsel can aid young entrepreneurs in confronting the challenges they will undoubtedly encounter and inculcate in them the significance of unwavering commitment. As you witness their development and triumphs, you'll witness your legacy persistently evolving through their accomplishments.

Creating a Positive Work Culture and Ethical Legacy

Beyond business success, your legacy can also be delineated by the work culture and ethical standards you foster within your organization. By nurturing an atmosphere of respect, inclusivity, and ethical conduct, you set a potent example for your employees and the broader business community. A workplace that esteems integrity, diversity, and employee well-being not only attracts top talent but also contributes to positive societal impact. When your employees feel valued, supported, and empowered, they, in turn, are more prone to make affirmative contributions to their communities and society as a whole.

Your ethical legacy transcends mere financial gains; it represents your commitment to conducting business in a manner that benefits both your stakeholders and the world. As you persist in leading by example, you motivate others to prioritize ethics and sustainability in their own ventures.

Embracing the Journey's Evolution

Your entrepreneurial journey is not stationary; it's an ever-evolving narrative with various chapters. Embrace the evolution of your journey with an open heart and a willingness to adapt to shifting circumstances. As you explore novel opportunities, confront fresh challenges, and celebrate fresh achievements, your legacy expands and opens new dimensions. Your unwavering determination remains the constant thread weaving through each stage of your journey, propelling you forward.

Giving Back to Your Community

As an entrepreneur, you wield the privilege of making a positive impact on your community. Beyond economic contributions, you can actively partake in philanthropic endeavors that support causes dear to your heart. Whether sponsoring local events, contributing to charitable organizations, or initiating community development projects, your commitment to giving back can forge a lasting legacy of social responsibility.

Furthermore, you can inspire others within your industry or network to join you in making a difference. Collaborative efforts with fellow entrepreneurs and businesses can amplify the positive impact you have on your community, generating a ripple effect of positive change.

Balancing Growth with Sustainability

Sustainability has emerged as a central concern in the business world.

Your journey should encompass a commitment to responsible and sustainable practices. Ponder how your business operations can minimize environmental impact, reduce waste, and contribute to a more sustainable future.

Customers and investors increasingly value businesses that prioritize sustainability. By aligning your growth with sustainability principles, you contribute to a healthier planet, enhance your brand's reputation, and appeal to socially conscious consumers.

Inspiring the Next Generation

Your entrepreneurial journey can serve as an inspiration to the next generation of aspiring business owners and leaders. Consider how you can actively mentor and support emerging entrepreneurs. Sharing your experiences, insights, and lessons learned can empower others to embark on their journeys with greater confidence and determination.

You can engage with educational institutions, participate in entrepreneurship programs, or even start initiatives aimed at nurturing young talent. By doing so, you contribute to the growth of future leaders who will continue to shape the business landscape.

Embracing the Challenges Ahead

Your entrepreneurial journey can serve as an inspiration to the next generation of aspiring business owners and leaders. While your journey has been marked by determination and success, it's essential to acknowledge that new challenges will arise. The business world is dynamic and unpredictable, but your unwavering commitment equips you to face whatever obstacles come your way. Embrace challenges as opportunities for growth and learning. Seek solutions with the same determination that has fueled your journey thus far. Remember that every challenge you overcome adds depth and resilience to your entrepreneurial story.

A Legacy of Endurance

Your unwavering determination has brought you to this point and will continue to guide you as you venture into the future. Your legacy is not just the story of your achievements; it's a testament to your enduring spirit and commitment to the ideals and values that drive you.

As you continue to write the chapters of your entrepreneurial story, know that your legacy will be a lasting one. It's a legacy of determination that inspires others, creates opportunities, contributes to society, fosters innovation, and promotes sustainability. Your journey is a powerful narrative of what is possible when one person remains resolute in the pursuit of their dreams.

Continued Growth and Adaptation

In the ever-evolving world of business, the path to success is not static.

Your journey will continue to evolve, and your unwavering determination will remain your compass. Stay attuned to market trends, emerging technologies, and changing consumer preferences. Adaptability will be key to maintaining your business's relevance and competitive edge.

Moreover, continue to invest in your personal and professional growth. Seek out new knowledge, expand your skill set, and stay curious. The more you learn and grow, the better equipped you'll be to navigate the challenges and opportunities that lie ahead.

A Never-Ending Journey

Your entrepreneurial journey is a demonstration of the power of determination and resilience. It's a narrative of triumph over adversity and a roadmap for future success. As you continue writing the chapters of your story, know that your unwavering commitment will be a source of inspiration, not only to those who follow in your footsteps but also to yourself.

Conclusion

As you continue your entrepreneurial journey, remember that it's not just about reaching a destination; it's about embracing the process and the growth that comes with it. Challenges will arise, but with unwavering determination, perseverance, adaptability, continuous learning, and a strong support system, you can conquer those challenges and achieve the success you've envisioned.

Your journey is a testament to your resilience, your commitment, and your ability to overcome obstacles. Embrace the lessons learned along the way, and let them propel you toward even greater achievements. The unwavering determination that has brought you this far will continue to guide you on the path to success. So, as you face each new chapter of your entrepreneurial story, do so with the knowledge that you have the inner strength and determination to overcome whatever challenges come your way. Your journey is a testament to the power of persistence, and your unwavering commitment will lead you to the triumphs that await on the horizon. Embrace the adventure, continue writing your unique story, and let your entrepreneurial spirit shine as a beacon of inspiration for others to follow.

Credits

Photograph: Jay Douglas

Makeup: Christian Alexander

Hair: Joanne Almond

Stylist: Sharon Spicer Evans

Becoming the Real Boss!

Becoming the Real

BOSS!

About the Author

"Becoming the Real Boss!" by Pamela Hogan is a comprehensive guide for aspiring entrepreneurs and seasoned business professionals. Drawing from her extensive experience of over 30 years as an entrepreneur and multiple business ventures, Hogan offers a roadmap to becoming a true boss in the competitive business world.

The book delves into the core elements of being a boss, emphasizing the qualities, skills, and mindset required to succeed. Hogan provides practical advice on navigating challenges, making strategic decisions, and building a solid professional presence.

"Becoming the Real Boss!" is not just a guidebook; it's a mentorship journey with a seasoned entrepreneur who shares candid insights, lessons learned, and inspirational anecdotes. Whether you're starting your entrepreneurial journey or seeking to elevate your leadership skills, this book equips you with the tools and mindset to thrive as a boss in the dynamic business landscape. Are you ready to embrace your full potential and become the real boss of your destiny

PAMELA D. HOGAN

PAMELA D. HOGAN

Made in the USA
Columbia, SC
20 June 2025

b76fd54d-ba55-415d-8b9a-01421bbf6084R01